IRANIAN CERAMICS

CHARLES K. WILKINSON

ASIA
HOUSE   DISTRIBUTED BY HARRY N. ABRAMS, INC.

I R A N I A N   C E R A M I C S is the catalogue of an exhibition selected by Charles K. Wilkinson, Curator Emeritus of Near Eastern Art at the Metropolitan Museum of Art and shown in the Galleries of Asia House as an activity of the Asia Society, Inc. to further greater understanding and mutual appreciation between the United States and the peoples of Asia.

An Asia House Gallery Publication/ all rights reserved
Printed in Japan by Book Craft Incorporated/ 1963
Distributed by Harry N. Abrams, Inc., New York

PREFACE

THIS BOOK, along with the exhibitions in the two small galleries of Asia House, attempts to display the character of Iranian ceramic art from the fourth millennium B.C. to the nineteenth century. Although some phases are not shown and others are represented by more than one example, it is to be hoped that these gaps and accents will not prevent appreciation of the flow of artistic merit through the ages. Enough, however, is here to demonstrate that the work of Iranian potters throughout the centuries is endowed with the particular Iranian character and that there is something for every taste. Its perfection is not that of cold precision. Its main qualities are warmth and liveliness. The sense of color, even when limited for technical reasons, is never lacking and often brilliant. Omar Khayyam would stay the potter's hand because the clay had once been man, but all can say that the potters of Iran could make clay live.

The author wishes to thank the several institutions and friends, who are listed at the end of this volume, for their help in making material available for this exhibition. In view of his recent tragic death, the name of Arthur Lane, late keeper of ceramics at the Victoria and Albert Museum, comes first. He was deeply interested in the pottery of Iran, and he had the ability to present serious study of Iranian ceramics in a reasonable and readable form. His are the best general books on the subject for the Islamic period. Miss Dorothy Shepherd of the Cleveland Museum, Miss Dorothy Minor of the Walters Art Gallery in Baltimore, Miss Margaret Gentles of the Art Institute of Chicago, Miss Carolyn Shine of the Cincinnati Art Museum, Mrs. Lois Katz of the Brooklyn Museum, and Miss Joan Rassieur of the Museum of Fine Arts in Boston all went to great trouble to make things available. The Metropolitan Museum of Art, the Cleveland Museum of Art and the Asia House Gallery have helped in the matter of color photography, special color transparencies having been made on very short notice. Richard Cleveland and Gordon Washburn have helped in every way, the former especially in the matter of installation, and the latter in making the necessary arrangements and encouraging me in this attempt to give people an opportunity to study an art in which the Iranians have excelled.

CHARLES K. WILKINSON

MAP OF IRANIAN CERAMIC SITES

USSR

☆ Kubachi

Bukhara ☆   Samarka ☆

☆ Tabriz

Caspian Sea

☆ Hasanlu

☆ Merv

☆ Ziwiyeh   ☆ Dailaman   ☆ Atrek
                              ☆ Gurgan
              Amul ☆   ☆ Sari

Nehavend ☆   ☆ Mazanderman   Nishapur ☆   ☆ Meshed
         Tehran ☆   ☆ Chasm-i-'ali
      ☆ Garrus   ☆ Rayy
      ☆ Hamadan   ☆ Saveh

            ☆   ☆ Sialk
      Sultanabad   ☆
                  Kashan   IRAN   AFGHANISTAN

            ☆ Isfahan

                                                                PAKISTAN...

☆ Yezd

☆ Susa

                        Kerman
                         ☆

☆ Shiraz
     ☆
Kast-i-abu Nast

IRAQ

                              Bandar 'Abbas
                                   ☆

                              PAKISTAN

Persian Gulf

SAUDI ARABIA

Gulf of Oman

INTRODUCTION

EARLY MAN, with his ability to make fire, found in clay a most remarkable and convenient substance. He has now used it for many millenia, and notwithstanding the invention in recent years of excellent new materials with which to make household utensils, it appears that mankind will continue to use clay and ceramic products for a long time to come. It must not be thought that clay vessels have been, or even are, used universally by men. Several races, such as the Eskimos, have been able to get along without them. None the less, clay is one of mankind's most useful servants, and in his employment of it he has shown great creativeness. He has used it to meet many different needs; in times of famine or fast, he has even been known to eat it. Here, however, we are concerned with his use of it to make earthenware. In doing this, he has exercised great art. He has developed, and sometimes lost, great technical skills for building up vessels by hand, for throwing and turning clay on the wheel, and for shaping it with molds, usually in conjunction with the wheel.

Clay, by its very nature, is an impressionable and malleable material, but when fired in the kiln it becomes more or less permanently fixed in the form given it, though the vessel is breakable. The shape, then, reveals to us the ability and the sense of design of the potter, no matter who he was or when he lived. The design is perpetuated whether it is a free and spontaneous one or a mechanical and clumsy one. When we look at even humble hollow ware, we find that we are in contact with the man who made it, no matter whether he be alive or long since dead. His work lives on for better or for worse.

It is because of this immediate perception irrespective of age that an exhibition of the ceramics of a single country, covering several millenia, has been arranged in Asia House. In this instance, the country chosen was Iran, or, as it is generally called in English literature, Persia, where pottery of superb quality was made for long ages. To those who have much archaeological knowledge, or who are learned in the history of design, it will be apparent that the pottery of other lands has influenced the ceramic art of this country. But this is far from saying that

[1]

Iranian pottery does not have its own character or that it did not in its turn influence that of other countries. What is clear is that certain characteristics distinguish it from the ceramic art of other lands. When thinking of Iran over such a long period, we must remember that during the centuries political boundaries were flexible, and a close adherence to the lines of the present-day map of Iran must be avoided. It must also be remembered that certain geographical and political names mean different things at different times.

Technical skill in building, and later in throwing and turning, has long been present in Iran, and this technical skill has been matched by the successful arrangement of designs to shapes of the vessels. The designs are often spirited drawings with an economy of line and skillful use of repetition, of emphasis, and of the unexpected. The beauty of some vessels is in the simplicity of their form and decoration, of others in their subtle complexity. One of the lessons to be learned by studying Iranian ceramics is that it is possible for completely different conceptions of design to exist and enjoy favor at the same time. For example, in the tenth century A.D. in the city of Nishapur, some potters were making simple and sparse designs while at the same time others were crowding on ornamentation, leaving no area undecorated.

Recent excavations at Tepe Sarab in the north of Kermanshah have produced examples of pottery earlier than any other hitherto known in Iran. Here, by the eighth millennium B.C. clay figures of animals and fertility goddesses were being made (see Braidwood, R.J., "The Agricultural Revolution" in *Scientific American,* September 1960, pp. 2–10). In this particular exhibition there is nothing so early as this, but certain early types of earthenware vessels of the fourth

Plate I

millennium B.C. are shown, such as that from Chasm-i-'ali near Rayy (1) where built pottery was decorated with designs painted in a pigment containing manganese and then fired in an oxidizing kiln so that the clay is red. Somewhat similar pottery has been discovered in other parts of Iran and in Turkestan. As early as the fourth millennium B.C., certain types of red or buff earthenware were decorated with repetitions of animals or birds combined with linear patterns (2).

Plate 2

They are so well designed that they still arouse our admiration. A feature of many of them is that a certain element—the horns of an animal, for example—is exaggerated in size or used as a decorative element without the beast itself being there. None the less, many animals are represented occasionally in a realistic way. The technique of burnishing was developed at an early date. This perhaps reached its highest point in the second millennium B.C. in the gray-black ware, on

[2]

which elaborate patterns were executed in this way, the most elaborate being that first found at Tureng Tepe near the Caspian Sea. This ware has since been discovered at Yarim Tepe and other places. Toward the end of this millennium, a fine burnished red ware was made that has been discovered near Gurgan. A fine example of this, a vessel with a long spout, has been lent by the Metropolitan Museum of Art (5).

Plate 5

Clay can be modeled with great ease, and it was used to make not only utilitarian vessels of many shapes, but also objects in the form of human beings, animals, or even travesties of such creatures. Indeed, these appear to be the first things made of clay. The Iranians were extremely inventive in making things of this kind, including vessels in the form of animals. The function of some of them we do not know, but it is hard to believe that they did not serve in some religious or cultic way. Although the significance of many of these may escape us, we are not prevented from enjoying or even disliking them as works of art. Many of them are striking in appearance and appeal to the taste of today (4, 6, 7, 8, 9). It is obvious to anyone who looks carefully and compares what he sees in the scope of this selection, and particularly if he studies Iranian ceramic art more fully, that there are many reiterations of similar ideas. Sometimes, perhaps, there are coincidences due to a similar state of mind; others may be due to unconscious influence or even deliberate copying.

Plates 4, 6 - 9

One of the great inventions associated with ceramic art was that of a vitreous glaze. This in all probability took place in Egypt, and in that country it was employed in the most dazzling fashion. An alkaline glaze was applied, not to natural clay, which presents certain difficulties, but to a gritty white body or to steatite, either of which is technically more satisfactory. Alkaline glaze does not appear in Iran until the second millennium B.C. At that time it was used at Susa, which is in the lowlands of Elam, near the southern part of present-day Iraq on the Iranian plateau. In the first millennium B.C., however, it does appear on the western side of Iran, not only in the south, but all the way north to Lake Urmia. Luristan, Kurdistan, and Azerbaijan have all produced examples.

In the seventh century B.C. glazed earthenware vessels were being made on the western side of Iran, to judge from the large number of glazed vessels of various kinds discovered in recent years. An example is a glazed rhyton in the form of an antelope head (13). Glazed bricks (15) played a great part in the decorations of Achaemenian palaces. The finest panels of these are preserved in the Louvre.

Plate 13 & 15

[3]

Plate 14

Plate 16

In later Parthian times, glaze continued to be used, though still only in the western part of the country. It was employed both for hollow vessels and for more sculptural purposes, as witness the finely modeled head, now in the Metropolitan Museum of Art, to which some gray glaze still adheres (14). During the Sasanian era glazed ware was either greenish blue or dark bluish green (19). Little of this has been discovered in Iran itself, except at Susa. It was very prevalent in Iraq, for example at Ctesiphon, which was an important center under Sasanian rule. Excavations by the Metropolitan Museum indicate that glazed ware was not made even in the Sasanian town of Shiraz, and so far no glazed objects of this period have been discovered in eastern Iran, the finest ware of that period being a burnished red ware (16). The center for fine glazed earthenware was obviously not in the Iranian plateau, and the success with polychrome glazes in Achaemenid times seems to have withered away until its revival in a new form in the early Islamic period. From then on, Iranians showed the greatest mastery in this art. This success did not come immediately with the Arab invasion but commenced with the ninth century of our era.

The first excavations that gave accurate information about Islamic pottery of this period were undertaken by the Germans before World War I at Samarra, a seat of Abbasid caliphate from 836 to 892. The greatest center for pottery in Iraq was probably Basra, and perhaps Bahgdad itself. Glazed earthenware was undoubtedly made in quantity before the actual foundation of Samarra. As far as Iran is concerned, glazed earthenware was not in general use until the early ninth century of our era, in spite of the examples like jars and rhyta from Ziwiyeh that have survived from the earlier periods. In this century, the art of glazing earthenware vessels with lead as a flux became extremely popular on the Iranian plateau, and this art also extended into what is now known as Uzbekistan, including Afrasiyab (Samarkand) and Tashkent. The excavations at Nishapur have revealed that in this century glazed vessels were used by a very large percentage of the population and not merely for palaces and the very rich. Ninth-century Iranian glazed earthenware was influenced by China, sometimes directly and sometimes indirectly by way of Iraq, which latter is not surprising, as Iraq was the seat of the Abbasid caliphate. This ware, however, soon developed its own characteristics. Two distinct types were involved, of which the first would seem to have originated to the west of Iran. In this, the clay, after it had been sun-dried, was covered with a lead glaze to which tin had been added. When fired in the kiln, this resulted in an opaque white glaze that entirely disguised the yellow or pinkish color of the earthenware body. In Iraq the white enamel was often decorated with dark blue from cobalt and a clear green from copper. We have no proof that this ware was made in Iran, but it was copied with some substitutions. For example, in Nishapur in the ninth century, manganese was substituted for the cobalt, so that the inscriptions normally in blue came out a purplish black (18). In the ninth century in Iraq polychrome luster painting was developed on this same opaque white glaze by refiring, but this was also beyond the scope of the Iranian potters at this time. In east Iran potters were influenced by the imported luster ware, but in their attempts to copy it, they used slip painting, and though this was a technique in which they were skilled, by its very nature it could not give the particular quality of metallic reflections.

Plate 18

Related to the opaque white wares of the ninth and tenth centuries was another of opaque yellow with green decoration. This was made generally in Iraq, in Iran, and in Uzbekistan, the example from Iraq being the finest in quality, though some of those from Nishapur are perhaps more entertaining in design (29).

Plate 29

Another major group at this time also shows signs of Chinese influence. In this, splashes of green, often supplemented by yellow-brown and purplish spots, tint the glaze. The Iranians quickly combined this with *graffiato* decoration, and they developed this in their own particular manner. This ware was made with a white engobe (over-all slip) to disguise the reddish color that the clay took on in the kiln. Because the glaze, with no tin in it, was transparent, this was important, as otherwise a good color scheme could not be effected. The ware continued to be made for several centuries, though it soon lost all resemblance to anything Chinese (32 and 35). Particularly striking examples are those from the Garrus, Aghkand, and Yastkand districts.

Plate 32 & 35

In the ninth and tenth centuries Khurasan and the districts extending from the southern shores of the Caspian east through Bokhara and Samarkand saw the emergence of a magnificent group of slip-painted earthenware. It is distinguished by an enveloping white engobe, on which was painted the decoration, often startlingly simple, but nonetheless extremely effective. Some of the finest pieces have merely simple inscriptions in Arabic (20 and 22). None are in Persian, though this ware was not made in the lands where Arabic was the native tongue. With the introduction of red, the designs are often more elaborate (23), and in some types the slip painting is superimposed in more than one layer (30). An olive green slip was sometimes used either in combination with other colors or alone, in which case, because a little chrome is in its composition, there is a

Plate 20 & 22

Plate 23 & 30

[5]

tendency to stain the glaze yellow. This can in some instances be considered as imitation luster, for the designs are related to those used in true luster, but in the east of Iran, some are of a type never seen in the west, as in an extraordinary bowl decorated with male and female figures (27). The combination of a black containing iron and another with chrome produced another type which may perhaps have been thought to serve as a substitution for luster. No. 29 is an example of this particular ware, which was made in great quantity in Nishapur and is peculiar to east Iran.

In that city one further type made throughout the ninth and tenth centuries deserves attention, although it never was exported to distant places. It is, as were all the slip-painted wares, underglaze painted and fired only once. Many examples, especially the cruder ones, have a buff ground; in the finer ones, there is a bone-colored engobe, and in many, an opaque mustard yellow covering much of the ground. The ware is remarkable for the human figures and strange beasts and birds with which it is decorated (21). It is certain that some of this ware was made specifically for Nestorian Christians, and it is more than likely that it was made by non-Muslims. It is a reminder that at this time there were still Christians, Jews, and Zoroastrians in cities such as Nishapur.

The successes of the ninth and tenth centuries did not entirely die out at the close of that time, but lingered on into the eleventh. Then, or in the twelfth century, there was a revolutionary change, and the latter century saw some of the Iranian potters' most extraordinary successes. This took place when the Seljuks were in power, and it continued after the Mongol invasion, which was the cause of so much destruction in the first half of the thirteenth century. The change was twofold, for both the body and the glaze were altered. It should be remembered, however, that unglazed earthenware, so practical for keeping water cool by evaporation, continued to be made no matter what kind of glazed pottery was being manufactured. It is still made.

The new glaze was in a way the re-invention—for so far no links have been discovered—of the alkaline glaze of antiquity, but this time with a mastery never achieved before. To fit this glaze, a new body was invented to take the place of natural clay, which is unsuitable for it. The new body was composed of quartz, to which ash and clay were added in small quantities and fused into a glassy composition. At its best, it is almost pure white. This alkaline glazed ware was made in many places, but certain types seem to have been restricted to one or two centers. For many of the bowls and shallow dishes, molds were

Plate 27

Plate 29

Plate 21

employed, a circular hole being in the center for the foot of the vessel. The alkaline glaze affected the color scheme in a major way, as blue, previously lacking in Iranian wares, now became prevalent, first from cobalt, not hitherto used there, although it was in Iraq, and second from copper, which now instead of producing a clear green made a fine turquoise blue. Green now played a very subordinate role, but sometimes a soft green was produced by introducing chrome in conjunction with copper, as in 39. This bowl, which is pierced, is an example of a type widely made, for it was produced in Rayy, Nishapur, Kashan and perhaps elsewhere. The holes filled with the glaze and produced transparencies, either colorless or colored dependent on the glaze. In the best pieces, the patterns are very graceful. The technique was combined with others, such as underpainting, and this in turn sometimes had designs scratched out to reveal the white beneath (57). At times, merely black underpainting is added, in some very boldly (42), thus reminding one of the black-and-white ware of the tenth century. This is not surprising, for this bold treatment was practiced in both techniques in Nishapur itself. Other pieces, made probably in Kashan (50), show a new elegance and decorative style. A number of vessels were made with a pierced outer shell decorated with underglaze painting, sometimes in more than one blue. The outstanding masterpiece of this kind is one now in the Metropolitan Museum of Art in New York (52), which has the added interest of being exactly dated (612 A.H./A.D. 1215). Closely related to these are others, underglaze painted in both black and blue, that are of great refinement, these also being made in Kashan. Coarser ones appear to have been made elsewhere, for example in Sultanabad and Sultaniyeh.

Plate 39

Plate 57
Plate 42

Plate 50

Plate 52

Underglaze painting was also associated with decoration in relief. The manufacture of this ware was not confined to one or two centers. Perhaps more interesting are the so-called "carved" wares which are often in monochrome, though not always so. They were mostly made in molds, among other places, in Nishapur, and were often, as some molds discovered there proved, of very high quality. New light was thrown on the process by the discoverey of a ceramic master model and also by clear evidence that these models were sometimes made of wood. The use of the mold made in one or more parts was highly developed at this time, and the potter made full use of this device, which enabled him to compete on more nearly equal terms with the metalworker. How closely the metalworker affected the potter is demonstrated here by two ewers, one in each medium (64 and 65).

Plate 64 & 65

[7]

Also under the Seljuks, the new arts were employed in the manufacture of tiles, bold inscriptions in blue glaze taking the place of the earlier ones which were of simple brick with cinnabar or blue-painted backgrounds.

To turn from the monumental to the exquisite, the twelfth century also saw a great flowering of the art of luster painting, which was practiced in both Rayy and Kashan. Although the Iranians cannot be credited with its invention, they developed it to a very high point of artistry, combining it with transparent color to obtain the richest effects, as for example in the tile from the Museum of Fine Arts in Boston (67). In the twelfth and thirteenth centuries the Iranian potters began to date their pieces, as they had not previously done. The earliest date known is on a lustered bottle from Rayy dated 575 A.H./A.D. 1179. Would that this practice had been more common ! Examples from both Rayy and Kashan show how great was the potter's skill at this time and how rich a decorative surface he could make (57–69). The potters of Kashan who made luster ware also made tiles, obviously designed for secular (69) as well as for religious purposes (66). Kashan was famous for making *mihrabs* (prayer niches), some of which are still in Iran, though others are now in museums, *in parte* or *in toto*. Many of these are elaborate constructions with flanking colonettes and with many inscriptions from the Koran. The luster is often heightened with touches of color. The art of luster disappears as far as we know in the fifteenth century and does not reappear until the seventeenth.

In the twelfth and thirteenth centuries luster was sometimes combined with another exquisite form of ceramic art, known popularly as *minai* (enamel) ware. A bottle from the Walters Art Gallery in Baltimore shows the two techniques combined—a good indication that they were both practiced in the same atelier (56). These polychrome vessels are fascinating both because they are fine examples from a technical point of view and also because they have lively drawings on them of men and animals. The color is almost always attractive, especially on those with an opaque blue (robin's-egg blue) ground. The subjects often consist of hunting or polo scenes. The technique became more involved, so that some pieces were further decorated in relief and gilding. Related to this ware is another usually known as *laivardina* from its deep blue ground. It was overglaze painted on the blue, with black, opaque, red, and gold leaf cut up into small pieces (71). Tiles were made in this fashion also. The fourteenth century ushered in some considerable changes. Elaboration, however, could hardly go further, and though some of the *minai* was still produced, its best days were over.

Plate 67

Plates 57 - 69

Plate 66

Plate 56

Plate 71

[8]

A very popular ware was one generally known as "Sultanabad," a great deal of which was probably made in Kashan. Some of poorer quality was made at Sultaniyeh, a seat of Mongol power southwest of the Caspian Sea. It is convenient to use the name Sultanabad merely as a label for this type, though as yet we have no exact proof of the area over which it was produced. The ware is not so gay as the luster and *minai* wares: its colors are more sober, with a less brilliant white, dark and light blue, turquoise, black, and often a warm gray. There is still elegance in the shapes and charm in the drawing of the animals and human figures (72). On the whole, the ware is delicate. Only occasionally is there strength in the main subject, as in the large bird in 74. The body of the ware is rarely as thin or as white as in the best twelfth and thirteenth century wares. Celadon wares, imported into Iran from the tenth century onwards, were now copied, though without the hardness of the originals (75 and 75a).

Plate 72 & 74

Plate 75

One can see that in spite of invasions by Turks and Mongols, which were major catastrophes, the ceramic arts of Iran continued on, not perhaps in the same form, but probably in one that was little different from what it would have been if these events had not taken place. All arts have their phases no matter how peaceful the conditions, and the only reflection perhaps to be seen here is the stressing of certain physical types, or of a peculiarity of costume. Iranian ceramic art continues to be Iranian, even in the next phase when once more the country was invaded, this time by Timur-i-lang—Tamurlane—and his mercenary forces. Following this event, there was a very close link indeed with China, and we know that Chinese wares were highly favored, as can be seen in the Persian miniature (79a, painted in the Timurid period in Shiraz about A.D. 1477.)

A collection with fourteenth-century pieces, which has survived in Ardebil and is now in the Tehran Museum, is a good example of Chinese influence. A dish belonging to Stuart C. Welch (79) is also an excellent example of blue-and-white ware which with some changes continued to be made in Iran for the next two centuries. This was a period in which Iranian cobalt was imported into China, because it was superior in quality to Chinese cobalt. For further indications of Persian influence on Chinese art from the eighth to the fifteenth century, see Basil Gray in *Iran*, Vol. I, 1963, pp. 13–18. An interesting example of how Chinese potters catered to Iranian trade is to be seen in 83, a blue-and white candle holder now in the Philadelphia Museum of Art. It dates from the early sixteenth century and is inscribed with Persian verses.

Plate 79

Plate 83

Although Persian feeling expresses itself even in these "imitations," it shows itself more clearly in other types from the fifteenth century on. A group known as Kubachi, named after a place in the Caucasus where many pieces were found intact, could never be mistaken for anything from China. The pieces are often bold, especially when underpainted in black under blue. Occasionally there is a dated piece to help guide us through this period. We are able, for example, to assign the strong blue glazed bowl underpainted in black to the fifteenth century. This type of ware was probably made in northeast Iran, the early center of Safavid power being at Tabriz. The capital was later moved to Isfahan, but our knowledge of what was made there in the way of ceramics is sadly lacking.

Plate 82 Elegant pieces such as the fine bowl shown in 82 show that there was again inventiveness. In this piece the attempt was made to combine several techniques. Many of the polychrome dishes of this time are charming in color and in mood, though some might be considerd effete.

There is no question, however, but that much of the Iranian glazed ware of this time, which for the past twenty or thirty years has been out of fashion, is well worth looking at. Granting that the tile work of the Timurid period possibly represents the highest point, to shut one's eyes to the tile work of the seventeenth and early eighteenth centuries is to miss a great deal of pleasure. Their charm is Plate 78 & 86 illustrated by two panels from pleasure pavilions (78 and 86). It is very likely, but by no means certain, that they were made in Isfahan itself. At this time there were potteries producing good glazed vessels in Meshed, Kirman, Yazd, Shiraz, and probably Kashan. Various types of ware were made in these cities. In Kirman attractive pieces were made with a celadon or blue ground with prettily drawn motifs, often of carnations, done in white with touches of blue and red. One strikingly bold tile has as a centerpiece a blue and white Chinese dragon. Plate 86 From Kirman too comes an elegant bottle, with blue cranes on its white surface and its intricate ornament contained within elaborately curved outlines (86). Plate 93 The *kalian* from the Victoria and Albert Museum is another outstanding seventeenth-century example (93). The potteries of Meshed are represented here by a large dish of blue and white, which with its carved design on the broad surrounding edge is very similar to one in the Victoria and Albert Museum (Lane, A., *Later Islamic Pottery*, 80B). Monochrome wares of this same century with relief decoration, which sometimes reflects Chinese motifs in anything but an accurate way, but which also is often pure Iranian, are of considerable charm. Plate 91 & 92 They are usually green or yellowish brown (91 and 92).

The late seventeenth and eighteenth centuries saw a revival not only of luster

[10]

ware, usually on a white or blue ground in monochrome luster (65), but also of *Plate* 65 thin porcelaneous white ware with transparencies. Sometimes decoration is carved on it. It is a renaissance of a ware very popular in the twelfth and early thirteenth centuries. It is possible to distinguish the earlier and later wares by the designs and by the foot, which is much heavier in the later version. It is sometimes known as Gombroon ware, Gombroon being Bandar 'Abbas, which was a port on the Persian Gulf. Occasionally the white ware is decorated with delicate patterns in black or black and blue.

During the nineteenth century, Iran was under the rule of the Kajar dynasty, and at this time there was strong European influence. In this century there were still Chinese imports with floral decoration in red, blue, and green with a bluish white ground, sometimes divided by "shields." The Persian versions, also painted in enamel colors, usually have yellow in addition. The ground is a truly white tin enamel. A goblet is also sometimes introduced into the scheme of decoration.

A typical expression of Kajar art is shown in a bowl in the Victoria and Albert Museum which can be dated precisely to 1851 (99). The difference be- *Plate* 99 tween this and the ceramics of the fourth millennium B.C. is great indeed in terms of time, in technique, and in feeling. Between them have been many styles, and it might be argued that there is no true continuity over this great length of time. None the less, all have come from Iran and were made by people living there, and perhaps it is as important to appreciate the differences as it is to recognize the similarities.

GLOSSARY

BASE: refers to the underside of a vessel

BOTTOM: refers to the inside of a vessel

BUILDING: using coils or slabs of clay to construct vessels usually without the use of a wheel

ENGOBE: a general covering of liquid clay (slip), white or colored

Graffiato: scratching through an engobe or slip to effect a linear decoration

LUSTER: an iridescent metallic effect of a golden or other hue obtained by the use of sulphur combined with silver oxide and copper oxide. Vessels made with luster decoration have to be fired a second time at a lower temperature.

Minai (enamel): a word given to a type of ware, also known as *haft rangi* (seven-colored). At the first firing pale blue, purple and green are incorporated. The supplementary colors—chestnut, white, black, red and leaf gilding—are overglaze painted necessitating refiring at a lower temperature. It is an elaborate technique confined to Iran in the 12th to the late 13th century. The ground is usually ivory white or robin's egg blue (color plate 63).

SLIP: sieved clay in suspension in water with the consistency of cream

THROWING: making shapes on the spinning wheel

TURNING: shaving down of a vessel on the wheel by means of a "rib" or tool

PLATES

1. BOWL
   Purplish black decoration on red
   Tepe Chasm-i-Ali, Rayy,
   4th Millennium B.C.
   Height 4 3/4"

2. JAR
  Buff with purplish brown decoration
  Sialk, mid-4th Millennium B.C.
  Height 13 1/4"

3. JAR
   Buff with purplish brown decora-
   tion
   Tepe Giyan, early 2nd Millen-
   nium B.C.
   Height 6 7/8"

4. VESSEL IN FORM OF AN
ANIMAL
Dark red
Dailaman, ca, 10th Century B.C.
Length 11"

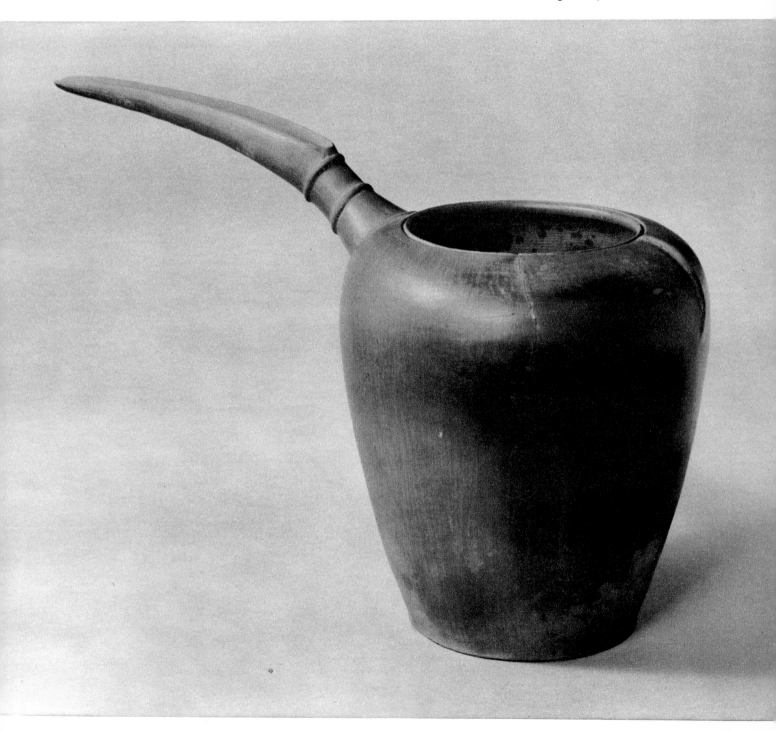

6. VESSEL IN FORM OF A
   HUMPED BULL
   Burnished red earthenware
   Dailaman, ca. 10th Century B.C.
   Height 14 3/4"

8. SPOUTED VESSEL
  Northwest Iran,
  ca. 10th Century B.C.
  Height 7 1/2"

9. STAG
  Red pottery
  Dailaman, ca. 10th Century B.C.
  Height 12 1/2"

10. PITCHER
Red decoration on pinkish buff
Sialk, 10th Century B.C.
Length 14"

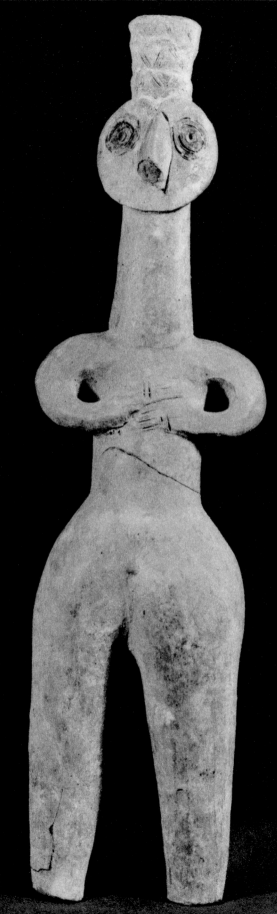

11. FEMALE FIGURE
Dailaman, ca. 900 B.C.
Height 19 1/2"

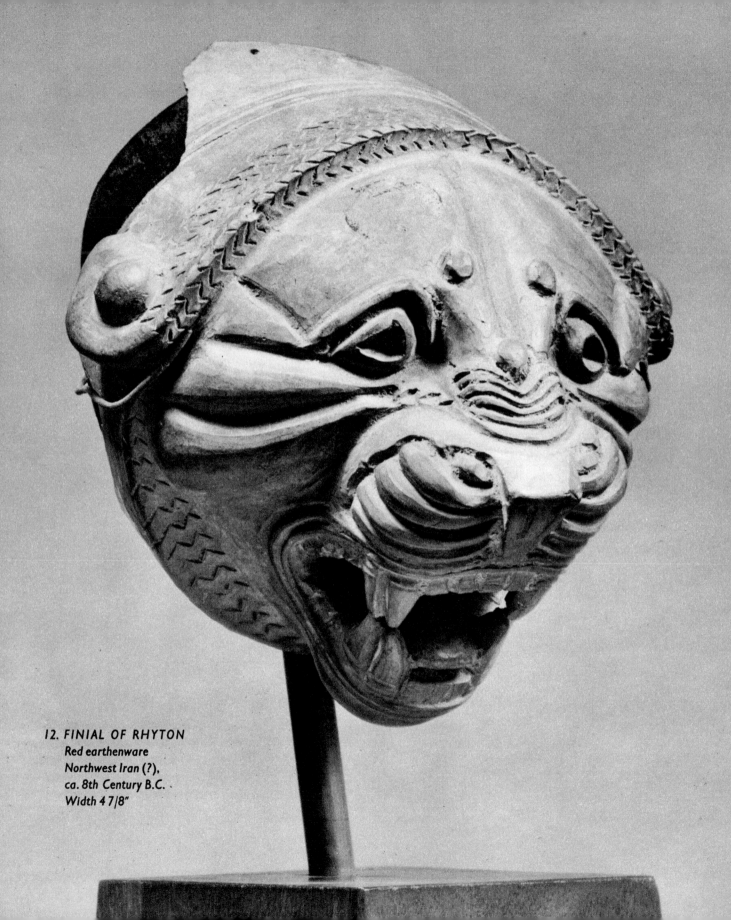

12. FINIAL OF RHYTON
Red earthenware
Northwest Iran (?),
ca. 8th Century B.C.
Width 4 7/8"

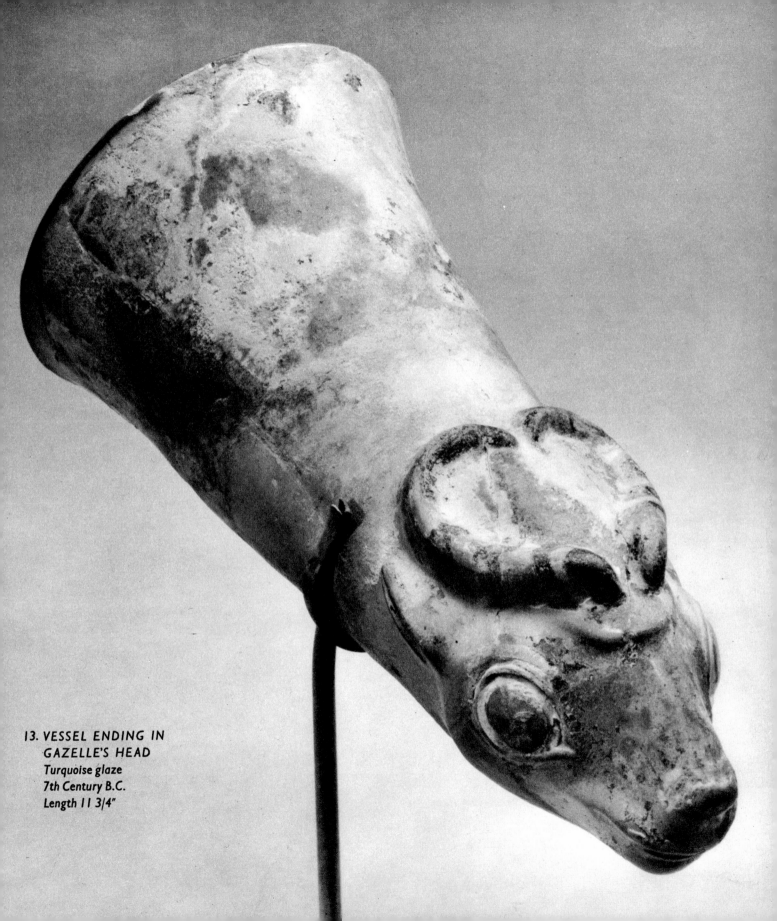

**13. VESSEL ENDING IN
GAZELLE'S HEAD**
Turquoise glaze
7th Century B.C.
Length 11 3/4"

14. HEAD FROM FOUNTAIN
Glazed earthenware
Parthian, ca. 2nd Century B.C.
Height 14"

15. GLAZED BRICKS
Susa, 4th Century B.C.
Height 10"

16. JAR
Burnished red earthenware
Sasanian, 7th Century A.D.
Height 14"

17. STORAGE JAR
Dark blue-green glaze
Sasanian or early Islamic,
7th/8th Century A.D.
Height 25 1/2"

18. *BOWL*
   Opaque white glaze, green and
   purplish black
   Nishapur, 9th Century
   Diameter 8 1/4"

19. BOWL
   Opaque yellow glaze with green
   Nishapur, 9th Century
   Diameter 8 1/4"

20. BOWL
Underglaze painted in black
white engobe
Nishapur, 10th Century
Diameter 9 1/2"

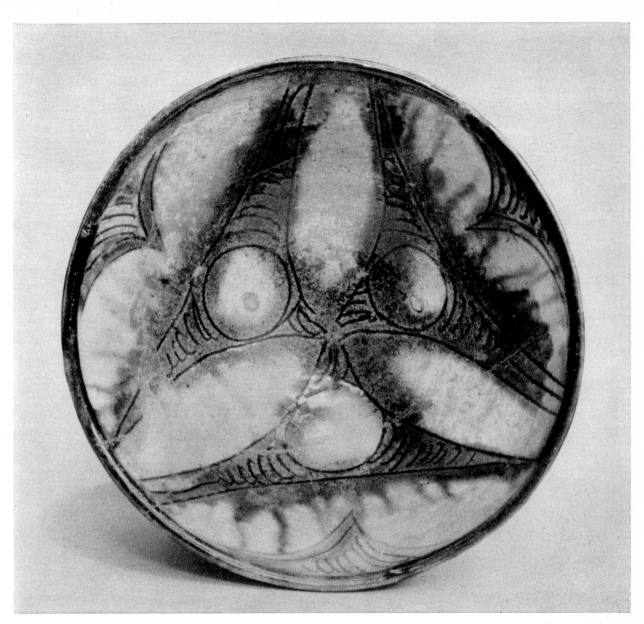

21. *DISH*
White engobe, graffiato drawing,
with splashes of green
Nishapur, 9th /10th Century
Diameter 6"

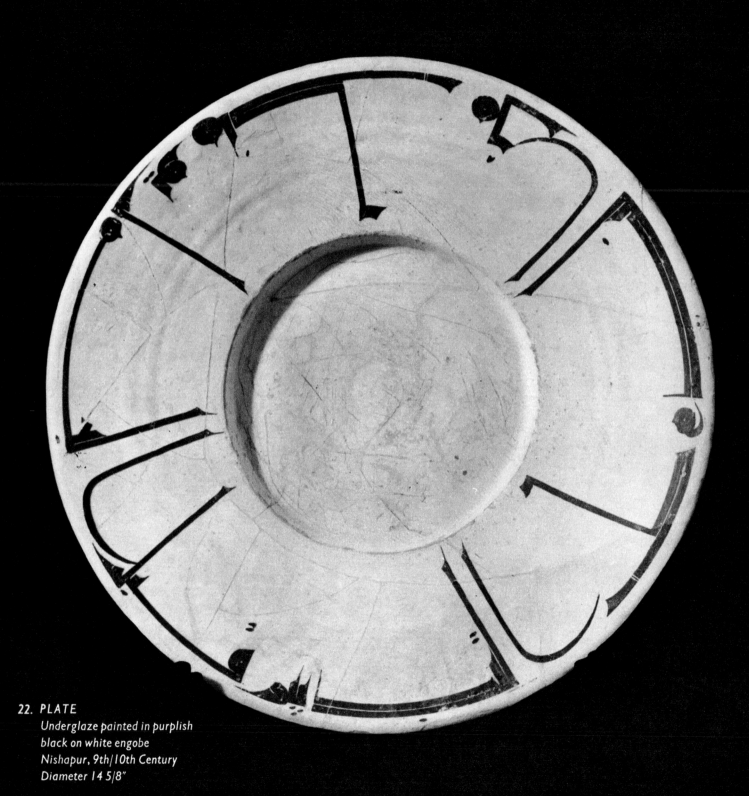

22. PLATE
*Underglaze painted in purplish
black on white engobe
Nishapur, 9th/10th Century
Diameter 14 5/8"*

23. BOWL
*Underglaze painted in purplish
black and red on white engobe
Nishapur, 10th Century
Diameter 7 7/8"*

24. BOWL
   Buff ware with underglazed
   painting in purplish black,
   yellow and green
   Nishapur, 10th Century
   Diameter 7"

25. JUG
Slip-painted in white on purplish
black engobe under greenish
lead glaze
Nishapur, 10th Century
Height 5 1/2"

26. BOWL
   Painted under lead glaze
   Nishapur, 10th Century
   Diameter 14"

27. BOWL
   Underglaze painted in olive
   green slip
   Nishapur (?), 10th Century
   Diameter 13 1/4"

28. BOWL
   Underglaze painted on white engobe
   Nishapur or vicinity,
   10th/11th Century
   Diameter 12 3/4"

29. **BOWL**
   *Underglaze painted brown-black
   and black staining the yellow
   glaze
   Nishapur, late 10th Century
   Diameter 9 1/4"*

30. BOWL
     Underglaze painted on white
     engobe
     Sari type, 10th Century
     Diameter 7 3/4"

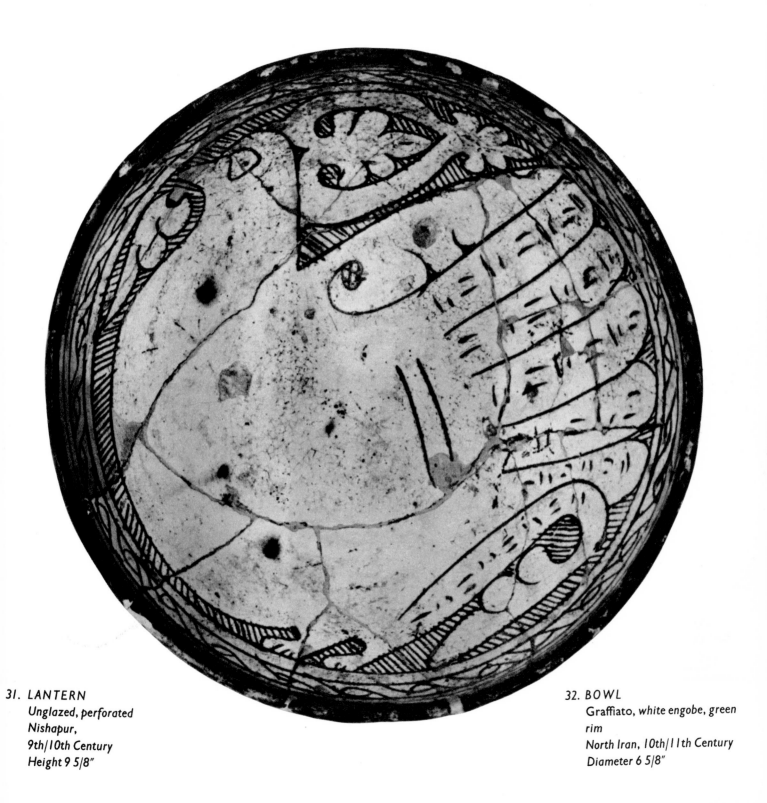

31. LANTERN
    Unglazed, perforated
    Nishapur,
    9th/10th Century
    Height 9 5/8"

32. BOWL
    Graffiato, white engobe, green
    rim
    North Iran, 10th/11th Century
    Diameter 6 5/8"

33. BOWL
   Graffiato, *white engobe, yellow-*
   brown streaks
   Yaskand, 10th/11th Century
   Diameter 7 3/4"

34. BOWL
   Graffiato on white engobe,
   green hatching spots and outlines
   Amol, 13th Century
   Diameter 11 1/8"

35. *BOWL*
   Champlevé, white engobe,
   green splashes and rim
   Garrus district, 12th Century
   Diameter 14 7/8"

36. BOWL
Champlevé, *green glaze*
Garrus district, 12th Century
Diameter 11"

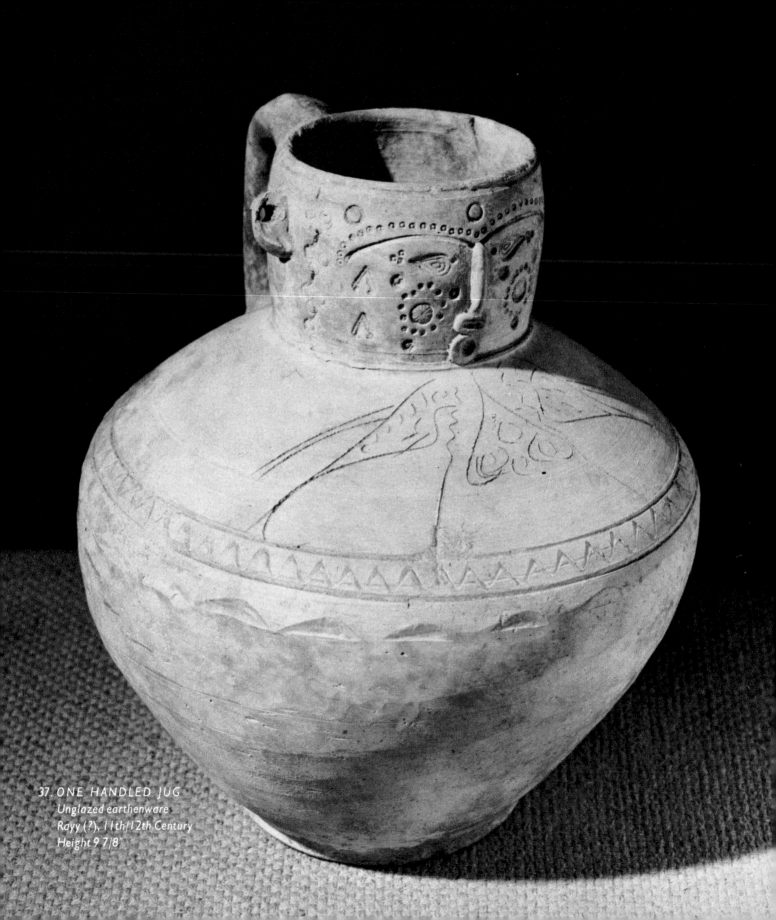

37. ONE HANDLED JUG
Unglazed earthenware
Rayy (?), 11th/12th Century
Height 9 7/8"

38. *FLOWER HOLDER*
    Graffiato under clear turquoise
    glaze
    Gurgan (?), 12th Century
    Height 8 3/4"

39. *BOWL*
   Graffiato with pierced trans-
   parencies, warm green glaze
   Rayy (?), 12th Century
   Diameter 7 1/2"

40. BOWL
Incised designs
Rayy (?), 12th Century
Diameter 6 1/4"

41. TANKARD
   Painted in black on relief under
   blue glaze
   12th Century
   Height 5 1/2"

42. TANKARD
*Black underglaze painted on
  relief decoration
12th Century
Height 6 1/2"*

43. *CUP*
   Molded with dark blue glaze
   Nishapur, Kashan (?),
   12th Century
   Height 3 1/2"

44. TANKARD
   Molded with dark blue glaze
   Nishapur, 12th Century
   Height 6 5/8"

45. DISH WITH FLAT RIM
  Polychrome on white ground
  So-called Lakabi, 12th Century
  Diameter 9 7/8"

46. LION
  Opaque turquoise-blue glaze
  13th Century
  Height 30"

47. TILE
   Opaque turquoise glaze
   13th/14th Century
   Height 9 1/2"

48. JAR
   Painted black,
   relief decoration under blue glaze
   Kashan (?), 13th Century
   Height 12 3/4"

49. WHITE BOWL
  Underglaze painted black and
  blue
  Late 12th/early 13th Century
  Diameter 7 7/8"

50. WHITE BOWL
   Underglaze painted black
   Late 12th/early 13th Century
   Diameter 8 3/8"

51. BOWL
   Pierced and painted black under
   blue glaze
   Late 12th/early 13th Centurly
   Diameter 8 7/8"

52. JUG
   Pierced outer shell,
   painted black under blue glaze
   1215/16 A.D.
   Height 8"

53. BOWL
   Painted black under clear blue
   glaze
   Late 12th/early 13th Century
   Diameter 10"

54. BOWL
   Painted black under clear blue
   glaze
   Early 13th Century
   Diameter 9"

55. PLATE
   Luster painted on white and blue
   Late 12th/early 13th Century
   Diameter 14"

56. BOWL
Luster painted
Late 12th/early 13th Century
Diameter 14"

57. CUP
Luster on white
Late 12th/early 13th Century
Height 5 1/8"

58. BOWL
Gold luster and blue on white
Mid-13th Century
Diameter 19 5/8"

. BOWL
Brown luster on white
609 AH/AD 1212
Diameter 8 5/8"

. FLOWER VASE
Overglaze painted in Minai
and luster
Late 12th/early 13th Century
Height 9"

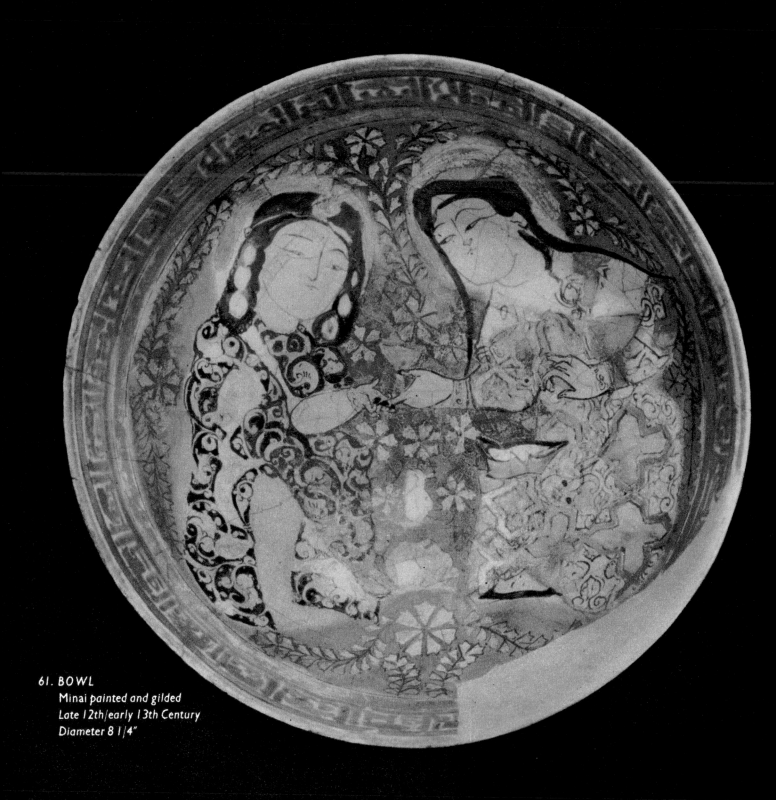

61. BOWL
Minai painted and gilded
Late 12th/early 13th Century
Diameter 8 1/4"

BOWL
Minai ware, overglaze painted
on white ground
Kashan, early 13th Century
Diameter 8 3/8"

63. BOWL
Minai ware, opaque turquoise
with polychrome overglaze
painting and gilding
13th Century
Diameter 7 3/4"

64. EWER
Bronze with some silver inlay
Height 11 5/8"

65. EWER
Luster and cobalt-blue decoration
Kashan, 13th Century
Height 12 1/2"

19.105.1

66. TILE FROM A MIHRAB
Luster, blue and green
13th Century
Length 15 3/4"

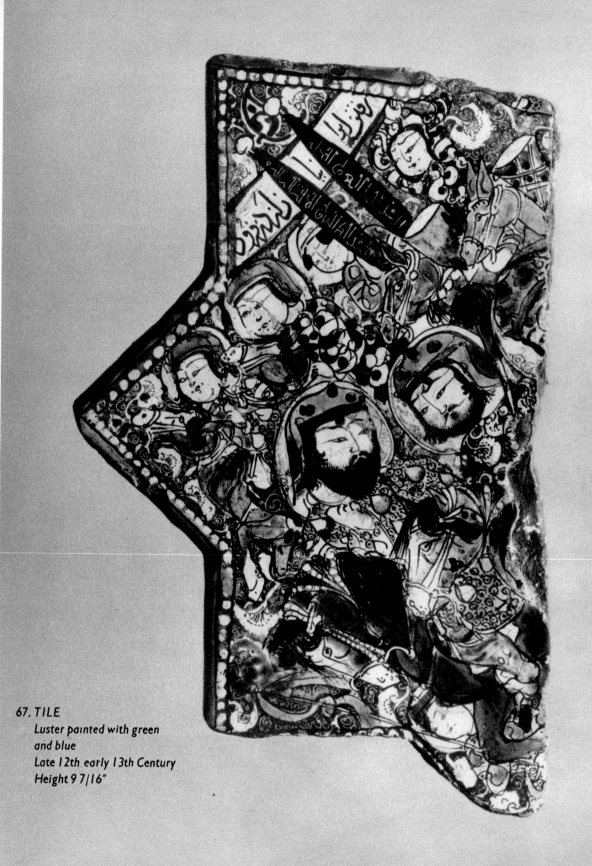

67. TILE
*Luster painted with green
and blue
Late 12th early 13th Century
Height 9 7/16"*

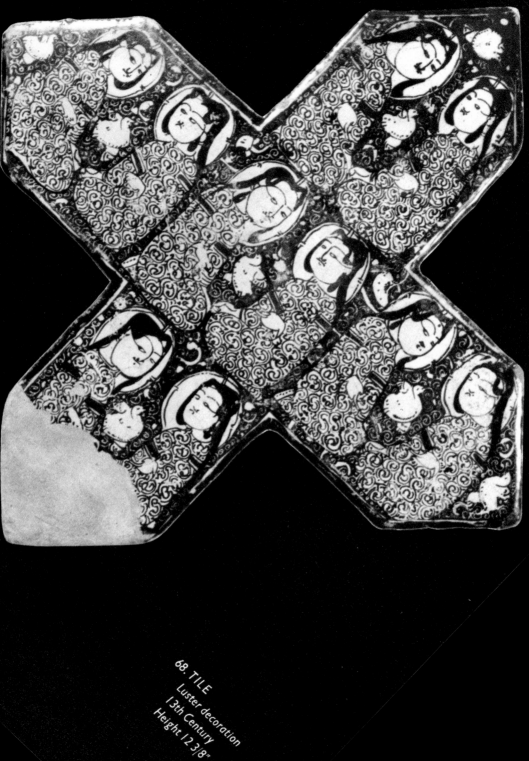

68. TILE
Luster decoration
13th Century
Height 12 3/8"

69. TILE
Decorated in luster and blue
14th Century
Height 8 1/8"

70. TILE
Minai with overglaze painting
and gilding
Kashan, 13th Century
Height 7 1/8"

71. ALBARELLO
Blue with overglaze painting
in white, red, and gilt
Late 13th Century
Height 14 3/4"

72. BOWL
   Painted black and blue under
   colorless glaze
   Sultanabad (Kashan?), early
   14th Century
   Diameter 6 3/8"

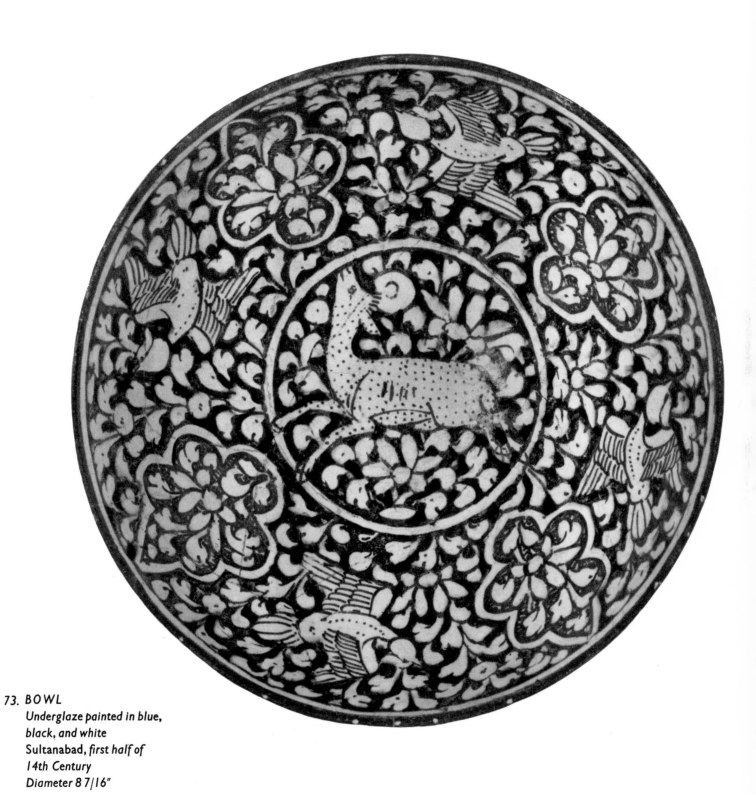

73. BOWL
*Underglaze painted in blue,
black, and white*
Sultanabad, *first half of
14th Century*
Diameter 8 7/16"

74. *BOWL*
   Beige-gray ground, white-slip
   painting, brown-black outlines,
   touches of cobalt blue
   14th Century
   Diameter 8 5/8"

75. BOWL
Imitation celadon, ribbed exterior
14th Century
Diameter 11 1/4"

76. BOWL
Kubachi ware, painted black
under blue glaze
North Iran, 15th Century
Diameter 12 3/8"

77. BOTTLE
Blue-and-white ware
15th/16th Century
Height 18 1/2"

78. DISH
Kubachi ware, blue-and-white
Northwest Iran, 16th/17th
Century
Diameter 12"

79. DISH
Blue-and-white ware
North Iran, 15th Century
Diameter 15 1/4"

80. DISH
   Kubachi ware, polychrome
   Northwest Iran, 17th Century
   Diameter 13"

81. DISH
Kubachi ware, polychrome
Northwest Iran, 17th Century
Diameter 13"

82. BOWL
    Kubachi ware, polychrome
    Northwest Iran,
    late 16th/early 17th Century
    Diameter 10 7/8"

83. CANDLE HOLDER
Blue-and-white ware
China, early 16th Century
Height 5 5/8"

84. *DISH*
Blue-and-white, incised band
near rim
Meshed, first half 17th Century
Diameter 17 1/2"

85. BOWL
   Blue-and-white, blue fawn on base
   17th Century
   Diameter 11 1/6"

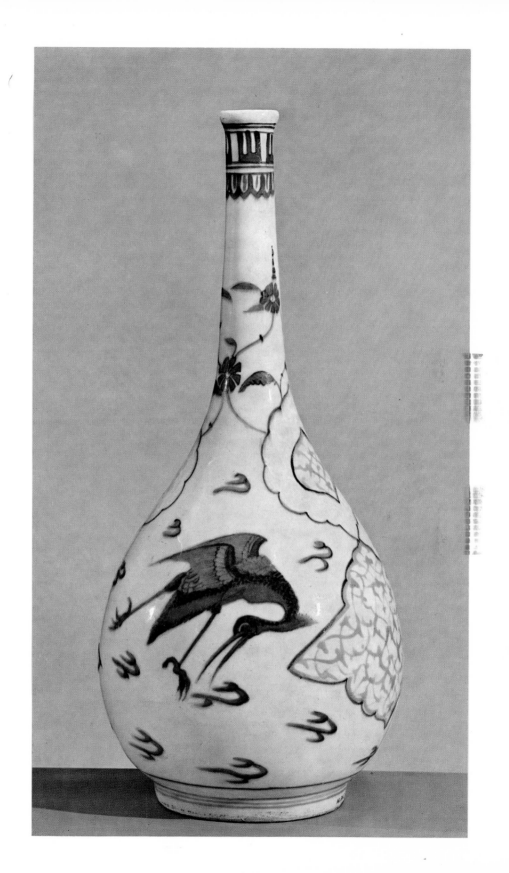

86. WINE BOTTLE
Polychrome on white ground
Kirman, 17th Century
Height 13"

87. PANEL OF TILES
  Polychrome
  Isfahan, 17th Century
  Length 6'6"

88. *TILES*
   Polychrome
   Isfahan, 17th Century
   Height 17 1/2"

89. *BOTTLE (KALIAN)*
   Blue with white and touches of
   ochre
   Kirman, dated 1658–9
   Height 11 1/2"

90. BOTTLE (KALIAN)
   White with blue, red, and
   olive green Kirman,
   second half 17th century
   Height 12 1/2"

91. WINE BOTTLE
   Green glaze over relief
   decoration
   Early 17th Century
   Height 14 3/8"

92. FLASK
Green glaze over relief
decoration
Early 17th Century
Height 8 5/8"

93. DISH
Celadon with white, center blue
and white
Kirman, 17th Century
Diameter 18 1/2

94. *BOWL*
   Slip-painted celadon with cobalt
   spots
   17th Century
   Diameter 9 5/8"

95. *WINE BOTTLE*
   Luster on blue glaze
   Second half 17th Century
   Height 10"

96. EWER
White incised ware
17th/18th Century
Height 9 5/16"

97. EWER
Luster on white
Second half 17th Century
Height 5 1/2"

98. BOWL
  White incised ware
  17th/18th Century
  Diameter 7 7/8″

99. BOWL
Polycrome enamel painted
Shiraz, dated 1846
Diameter 16 3/8"

CATALOGUE NOTES

1. BOWL
    Purplish-black decoration on red
    Tepe Chasm-i-ʿali, Rayy, 4th millennium B.C.
    Height: 4 3/8"
    Museum of Fine Arts, Boston

A feature of this particular ware is the use of animal motifs. In this example the head and the horns are supplemented with a bold herring-bone pattern. In other vessels from the same site the design is composed only of a series of pairs of horns arranged in bands. Much of this ware shows connections with a type known as Sialk 2. Tepe Sialk is a site that has been so extensively excavated that it has yielded a sequence of early Iranian pottery over a long period of time. It might be added that this site is not far from Kashan, one of the most, if not the most, important city in Iran for the manufacture of ceramics in Islamic times.

2. POT
    Painted in brownish black on buff
    Tepe Sialk, mid-4th millennium B.C.
    Height: 13 1/4"
    Dr. and Mrs. William K. Simpson

The painted earthenware of the 4th millennium B.C. is often outstanding for its high quality, its pleasing shapes, and its excellent surface design. The animals or birds that frequently form decorative bands around these vessels could not be more skillfully designed. On occasion the horns, the tail, or the ears of the animals are greatly exaggerated in size or treated in a fantastic manner. This emphasis is sometimes almost humorous. In general, the drawings are both decorative and endowed with life.

3. JAR
    Buff with purplish-brown decoration
    Tepe Giyan, early 2nd millennium B.C.
    Height: 6 7/8"
    Museum of Fine Arts, Boston
    Gift of Nazarte Aga

A feature of this type of ware is the combination of birds and "sun disks." A peculiarity of this particular jar is the representation of what would appear to be a building of some nature. The cross-hatching suggests it was made of woven reeds, but this visual suggestion may well be misleading.

[117]

4. VESSEL IN THE FORM OF AN ANIMAL
   Dark red earthenware
   Dailaman, about 10th century B.C.
   Length: 11″
   Metropolitan Museum of Art
   Gift of Mr. and Mrs. Lester Wolfe
The treatment of the mouth is similar to that of the vessels in the form of humped cattle generally known as coming from Amlash.

5. SPOUTED JAR
   Burnished red ware
   North Iran, ca. 10th century B.C.
   Length: 16 1/2″
   Metropolitan Museum of Art
This vessel is a remarkably fine specimen of the potter's skill, for it is extremely well and thinly turned. The ware is light, and the form elegant. There is a vestigial tail, so to speak, that is slightly reminiscent of the tails to be seen on vessels from Amlash (Dailaman). It is possible, however, that this vessel was made on the southeastern side of the Caspian Sea. A terra-cotta figure in the Archaeological Museum, Tehran, shows a long, spouted, handleless vessel of a different shape being held between both hands on a level with the face. This figure suggests that the use of such vessels was of a ritualistic nature (*see* A. Godard in *Athar è Iran*, vol. III, 1938, p. 262, Fig. 182).

6. VESSEL IN THE FORM OF A HUMPED BULL
   Burnished red earthenware
   Amlash (Dailaman), ca. 10th century B.C.
   Height: 14 3/4″
   Nazli Heeramaneck, New York
The variety among these vessels is extraordinary. In this instance the hump and head are treated as one tapering cylindrical form. Presumably the orifice in the top of the hump is for filling the vessel. The mouth is no longer a true mouth but a channel projecting beyond a small orifice. There is no indication of a tail. At Marlik Tepe the Iranian Archaeological Service found pottery humped bulls in earthenware and also some of bronze mounted on four wheels. (*See Illustrated London News*, May 5, 1962.)

7. VESSEL IN THE FORM OF A HUMPED BULL
   Amlash (Dailaman), ca. 10th century B.C.
   Length: 12 1/2″
   Nazli Heeramaneck, New York
The example is one of the most striking of the many bulls of this type found in the province of Dailaman. There is but one orifice which is the spoutlike mouth. The two ears are pierced and there is a loop that joins the back of the head to the front of the hump. The tail is wedge-shaped.

[118]

8. SPOUTED VESSEL

Warm gray unglazed earthenware with incised decoration
Northwest Iran, ca. 10th century B.C.
Height: 7 1/2"
Mr. and Mrs. John de Menil

This vessel, which is suggestive of designs by Hieronymus Bosch, is reputed to have been discovered to the southwest of the Caspian Sea. From this region small boots with no surmounting vessel have also been unearthed. Larger ones have been found in Hasanlu, in Azerbaijan, and across the Russian border. This vessel has these and also scratched triangles around the rim.

9. VESSEL IN THE FORM OF A DEER

Red pottery with incised decoration
Dailaman, ca. 10th century B.C.
Height: 12 1/2"
M. Mahboubian, New York

The vessel has but one orifice which leads to the spoutlike mouth. One can but speculate on the problem of the function of these zoomorphic vessels and the meaning of their exaggerated forms.

10. PITCHER

Pinkish earthenware decorated with designs in red
Sialk, 10th century B.C.
Length: 14"
Nazli Heeramaneck, New York

Vessels of this type were found by French archaeologists in great numbers at Tepe Sialk near Kashan. (*See* R. Ghirshman, *Fouilles de Sialk*, vol. I, 1938; vol. II, 1939.) The decoration around the root of the spout suggests a feature of the metal pitchers of the same date in which the spout was fastened to the body by studs through a circular boss. The base of this pitcher is decorated with a cross as is often the case with this ware.

11. FEMALE FIGURE

Earthenware with eyes painted black
Amlash (Dailaman), ca. 900 B.C.
Height: 19 1/2"
K. Rabenou Ltd., New York

A number of these large female figures have been discovered, not always with blackened eyes. All have the curious, masklike face, the triple-tiered crown, and elongated neck. The ears are pierced, and a similar figure in an Iranian collection has a gold earring still intact. Vessels, somewhat resembling feeding cups with a spout, are also decorated with similar masklike faces and triple-tiered headresses. (*See* N. Terrace, E.L.B. in *Syria*, 1962, p. 214, Fig. 4.) Published: *Catalogue of Arts Club of Chicago.* Similar in catalogue of *700 Ans d'art Iran*, Paris, 1961.

12. LION HEAD, FRAGMENT OF A VESSEL

Hard, red earthenware

Northwest Iran, ca. 700 B.C.

Width: 4 7/8″

Nazli Heeramaneck, New York

The modeling of this lion's head shows strong Assyrian influences, but the treatment of the hair ending in curls, that can also be considered ears, has affinities with the metal-work of Luristan, especially in the case of certain disks ornamented with human heads. A very similar peculiarity is to be seen on some of the gold work discovered in Ziwiyeh in Persian Kurdistan. In this same site many glazed earthenware vessels ending in animal heads were unearthed. A common practice in the Near East at this time was to make drinking and larger vessels of this animal-headed type. Published : A.U. Pope, *Masterpieces of Persian Art*, 1945, Pl. 21a.

13. VESSEL ENDING IN GAZELLE HEAD

Reddish ware covered by turquoise glaze

with touches of white and near black

Ziwiyeh area, Kurdistan, 7th century B.C.

Length: 11 3/4″

Metropolitan Museum of Art, Rogers Fund

This is one example of the many glazed vessels found in this area. Some are of simple ovoid shape with a circular neck and rim, others, such as this example, end in animal heads. Some are small and were used for drinking; the larger ones, such as this, were for replenishing the empty cups. Published: C. K. Wilkinson, The Metropolitan Museum of Art *Bulletin*, April, 1960, p. 298, Fig. 33; H. Hoffman, "The Persian Origin of Attic Rhyta" in *Antike Kunst* 4 (1961) Heft 1, p. 24 and Pl. 12, 4.

14. HEAD FROM A FOUNTAIN

Glazed red earthenware

Parthian, ca. 2nd century B.C.

Height: 8 1/2″

Metropolitan Museum of Art, gift of Walter Hauser

The head has a cylindrical orifice at the mouth indicating its use. The glaze has almost totally disappeared and is of the same gray color as that on glazed water bottles excavated at Susa. The beard is decorated with iron pyrites. The custom of using insets of this kind in the beard goes back to the 3rd millennium. The modeling of the features is much superior to that of most Parthian heads found in Iran.

15. GLAZED BRICKS

Greenish blue, white, and yellow outlined in purplish black

Susa, Southwest Iran, 4th century B.C.

Combined height: 10″

Metropolitan Museum of Art, acquired by exchange, Archaeological Museum, Tehran, 1948

These three bricks made of a gritty body once formed part of the border of a frieze at the palace of Artaxerxes II at Susa. Although we know that workers from Babylon were imported for making such bricks, the technique differs here in that the outlines are built up high with manganese-colored clay between the colored areas.

[120]

16. JAR

Burnished red earthenware with incised decorations
Kasr-i-abu Nasr, near Shiraz, 7th century A.D.
Height: 14″
Metropolitan Museum of Art, Rogers Fund

Sasanian pottery made in Iran is, as far as is known, not of very high quality. Judging by the Metropolitan Museum's excavations near Shiraz, most of it was heavy and aesthetically unappealing. Occasional vessels, such as this, have dignity if not refinement.

17. STORAGE JAR WITH THREE HANDLES

The decoration is in relief under a dark blue-green glaze
Probably from Susa, 7th-8th century A.D.
Height: 25 1/2″
Mr. and Mrs. Arthur Babakhanian, New York

Glazed pottery of this type was very common in Mesopotamia and never seems to have been made on the high plateaus of Iran. The Sasanian storage jars excavated at the Sasanian-Islamic site of Kasr-i-abu Nasr near Shiraz were all unglazed. Large jars of the kind seen here have been found in Susa, and one example is in the Louvre.

18. BOWL

Opaque white glaze with overglaze splashes of green and inscription in purplish black
Nishapur, 9th century
Diameter: 8″
Metropolitan Museum of Art, Rogers Fund

This type of ware was made in Nishapur in great quantity. It was copied from the opaque white ware of Mesopotamia but, due to the lack of cobalt at that time in Nishapur, manganese was substituted, giving a purplish black instead of the dark cobalt blue.

19. BOWL

Opaque yellow glaze with overglaze decoration in green
Nishapur, 9th century
Diameter: 8 1/4″
K. Rabenou, New York

Many bowls of this rather heavy type were made in Nishapur in the 9th and 10th centuries though few of them were so elaborately decorated as this. The commonest form of decoration consists of circular groups of spots, broad arrows, and splashes of green.

20. BOWL

Underglaze painted in brownish black on white engobe on reddish body
Nishapur, 10th century
Diameter: 9 1/2″

This particular type of black-on-white ware, distinguished by the word *Ahmad* in the bottom, was made in great quantity in Nishapur. Although it lacks the precision of the writing to be seen in plates such as 21, the freedom of execution has its own charm. The base is beveled and does not have a true foot ring.

21. DISH

Reddish earthenware with white engobe,
graffiato *design with splashes of green in the near colorless glaze*
Nishapur, 9th-10th century
Diameter: 6″
Mr. and Mrs. Lester Wolfe, New York

Enormous quantities of this ware, often with the addition of yellow-brown and purplish black to the color scheme, were made in Mesopotamia, Iran, and Uzbekistan in the 9th and 10th centuries. They were glazed imitations of Chinese wares of the T'ang period. In Nishapur some fragments of the Chinese originals were excavated by the Metropolitan Museum of Art.

22. PLATE

Underglaze painted in purplish black on white engobe under colorless glaze
Nishapur, 9th-10th century
Diameter: 14 5/8″
City Art Museum, St. Louis

This plate is one of a group of which the sole decoration consists of an elegantly drawn inscription in Kufic writing. These inscriptions are in Arabic and seem always to be moral adages. This one, translated by Dr. Ettinghausen, reads: "Deliberation before work protects you from regret." Published: L.O. Nagel, "Some Middle Eastern Ceramics in the City Art Museum, St. Louis" in *Oriental Art*, vol. IV (1958), p. 116, Fig. 2.

23. BOWL

Underglaze painted in purplish black and tomato red on white engobe
Nishapur, 10th century
Diameter: 7 7/8″

Many bowls of this type have been unearthed in Nishapur. They are remarkable for the fineness of their potting, their well-formed foot rings, and the absence of color in the glaze. The whole of the vessel is covered with engobe and the glaze extends to the base.

24. BOWL

Buff ware with underglaze painting in purplish black, yellow, green, and carnelian red
Nishapur, 10th century
Diameter: 7″

Buff ware, so called because it is the characteristic color of the ground, was one of the most popular in Nishapur. Only rarely is a white engobe added. The cross on the bowl may or may not have Christian connotations, but this type of ware was made for, if not by, Nestorian Christians, though not necessarily for them exclusively. The exterior is decorated.

25. JUG

Slip-painted in white on purplish-black engobe under greenish lead glaze
Nishapur, 10th century
Height: 5 1/2″
Metropolitan Museum of Art, Rogers Fund

This type of slip-painted ware with many variations, such as white on brown and yellow on brown, was easily affected by changing the color of the engobe and of the glaze. In some instances, the glaze, instead of being greenish as here, is a full clear green. Wasters from kilns were discovered in Nishapur, but vessels of this ware were also made in Afrasiyab (Samarkand).

26. BOWL

Painted yellow, purplish black, and green on buff under lead glaze
Nishapur, 10th century
Diameter: 14″
Cleveland Museum of Art, purchase from the J.H.Wade Fund

The bowl is a particularly fine example of a ware peculiar to Nishapur. The scene consists of two bearded men, sitting on stools, their divided cloaks or scarves descending almost to the ground. Between the men are two other men in high boots who give the impression of dancing but who are sitting cross-legged. The central panel recalls the great horseman bowl, in which the horseman is accompanied by a cheetah-like creature, found in Nishapur by The Metropolitan Museum of Art and now in the Tehran Museum. This bowl has the horse and cheetah (?) too, but the horseman has disappeared. On the ground in several places is the word *barakeh* (blessing). Published: D.G. Shepherd, "Bacchantes in Islam," *The Bulletin of the Cleveland Museum of Art*, vol. XLVII No .3, March, 1960, pp. 42–49.

27. BOWL

Underglaze painted in olive-green slip on white engobe
Nishapur (?), 10th century
Diameter: 13 1/4″
Nazli Heeramaneck, New York

This extraordinarily modern-looking bowl is one of a group made in imitation of luster. In this example, however, even more than in some others, the potter has gone far beyond imitation. The whole of the exterior is glazed including the entire base.

28. BOWL

Underglaze painted in black, red, green, and yellow on white engobe
Nishapur (?), 10th-11th century
Diameter: 12 3/4″
Heeramaneck Galleries, New York

Several bowls of this type have reputedly been found in Nishapur. The Metropolitan Museum's excavations yielded none, but some related pieces indicate this group could well have been unearthed in that great site. A bowl of similar ware, now in The Cleveland Museum, shows some connections with the Nishapur buff ware (see 27), but whether this ware, painted on a white engobe, was also made there is by no means certain.

29. BOWL
   Underglaze painted in brown black and black with chrome on a white engobe
   Nishapur, Late 10th-11th century
   Diameter: 9 1/4"
   Seattle Art Museum, Eugene Fuller Memorial Collection
The use of chrome appears to have been introduced by the Nishapur potters in the 10th century. Just enough is added to the black to tinge the lead glaze a transparent yellow. The ware appears to have been exceedingly popular and the ornamentation varies greatly. In many examples the decoration consists merely of a band of simulated Kufic writing.

30. BOWL
   Underglaze painted on white engobe in olive green, red, and purplish black
   Mazanderan (Sari ?), 10th century
   Diameter: 7 3/4"
   Metropolitan Museum of Art, Rogers Fund
In Gurgan, Sari, in other places near the Caspian Sea, and in Nishapur and Turkestan the technique of superimposed slip-painting was successfully practiced. Birds and stiff flowers were particularly popular in Sari, Amol, and Gurgan. They were not made in Nishapur, though occasionally imported there.

31. LANTERN
   Unglazed and perforated earthenware
   Nishapur, 9th-10th century
   Height: 9 5/8"
   Metropolitan Museum of Art, Rogers Fund
Lanterns with perforations were used to carry small lamps with pinched spouts. The lamps themselves were usually filled with mutton fat rather than oil. Lanterns of this type were also glazed, though none was unearthed at Nishapur.

32. BOWL
   Graffiato *on white engobe over reddish body. Glaze at the rim colored green*
   North Iran (Rayy ?), 10th-11th century
   Diameter: 6 5/8"
   Charles D. Kelekian, New York
A group of vessels with *graffiato* decoration usually consisting of one or more birds is reputed to have come from Rayy. There is, however, no proof they were made there. Characteristic of the group is the green rim. The fine work of the interior contrasts with the crudely turned exterior. In this particular bowl there are splashes of green and purplish color on the outside near the rim. The bowls of this group have a concave base and no foot ring.

33. BOWL

Graffiato *decoration on white engobe, yellow-brown streaks*
Yaskand, 11th-12th century
Diameter: 7 3/4"
Metropolitan Museum of Art, Rogers Fund

The decoration has been effected by cutting through the white engobe and applying iron oxide to those areas. This has left the Kufic inscription of good wishes in white against a dark brown ground. The streaks are due to the running of the iron-stained glaze as the bowl was fired. The three "spur" marks show that a smaller vessel was fired within this one—a common Iranian custom. The base is concave, buff in color, and unglazed.

34. BOWL

Warm white engobe, decorated in graffiato *and with warm green spots, crosshatching, and outlines*
Amol, 13th century
Diameter: 11 1/8"
Metropolitan Museum of Art

The outside of the bowl is smooth, unglazed, and dark red in color. The engobe covers the vertical rim, the top of which is green. A number of bowls and dishes of this type have come from Amol. Though many of them are more fantastic than this, few have the lightness of touch to be seen in the drawing of the birds.

35. BOWL

Champleve, *white engobe, green splashes on rim*
Garrus district, 12th century
Diameter: 14 7/8"
Art Institute of Chicago, Kate S. Buckingham Fund

From the Garrus district have come many large bowls such as this. They have in common a red body, usually poorly turned, and a band of green glaze near the rim on the exterior. The animals, though often with fierce faces, have rather boneless bodies. More spirited drawing is to be seen in the scrolls and foliate forms of the background. Other bowls are decorated with inanimate forms, including a debased form of Kufic.

36. BOWL

Champleve, *with green glaze over engobe*
Garrus district, 12th century
Diameter: 11"
Museum of Fine Arts, Boston

Some of the bowls from the Garrus district are in monochrome, green being the favored color. These vessels are sometimes ascribed to Yaskand, as are those of the type shown in 35.

37. ONE-HANDLED JUG

Unglazed earthenware with modeled, impressed, and graffiato *decoration*

Rayy (?), 11th-12th century

Height: 9 7/8″

Philadelphia Museum of Art

This jug, of porous earthenware for keeping water cool, is particularly interesting in that the free drawing of the *graffiato* birds is remarkably like that painted on bowls found in Rayy. The style is unlike that of the Mesopotamian unglazed jars decorated with human heads and human figures.

38. FLOWER HOLDER

Graffiato *under clear turquoise alkaline glaze*

Gurgan (?), 12th century

Height: 8 3/4″

K. Rabenou Ltd., New York

This type of vessel was made in Rayy, Nishapur, and in many other places in the 12th century. It was later made with other techniques throughout the centuries, some very attractive examples being made with luster decoration in the 14th and 18th centuries.

39. BOWL

Graffiato *with pierced transparencies, composed gritty body, and warm green alkaline glaze*

Rayy (?), 12th century

Diameter: 7 1/2″

Metropolitan Museum of Art, bequest of William Milne Grinnell

Such bowls were made in one-piece molds, and are often extremely thin and attractive. Although many were made in Nishapur, no other of this color has been excavated there.

40. BOWL

Incised decoration on the exterior of the gritty gray-white body
  under a soft purplish alkaline glaze. The interior is glazed turquoise blue

Rayy (?), 12th century

Diameter: 6 1/4″

Metropolitan Museum of Art, bequest of William Milne Grinnell

The design is basically that of the green glazed bowl (39). The free drawing, combined with the softness of the coloring, makes this type of ware exceedingly attractive. The lack of precision in Iranian ceramics can often be a positive virtue.

41. TANKARD

Painted in black on relief decoration under clear blue glaze

12th century

Height: 5 1/8″

Cleveland Museum of Art, Edward L. Whittemore Fund

The motif of animals running after each other was often used on circular vessels in the 12th century. It appears on a luster piece dated A.D. 1179 found in Rayy and on a number of metal ewers. No motif of this type has been drawn with greater verve than this. Published : *Handbook*, The Cleveland Museum of Art, 1958, No. 700.

[126]

42. TANKARD

> Champleve *colored black on white*
> *Nishapur (?), 12th century*
> *Height: 6 1/2"*
> *University Museum, Philadelphia*

Since the Metropolitan Museum gave up its concession at Nishapur, excavations have been pursued on a commercial basis. Wasters and molds that are now in the Archaeological Museum and are credited as having come from Nishapur have extended the number unearthed by the Metropolitan Museum's expedition. Among the later finds are some of this black-and-white ware. It is interesting to see that the famous black-and-white underglaze painting did not die out with the Samanids, but was continued in Seljuk times. In this example, both body and glaze are different, but we can see that the love of bold design and contrast did occasionally survive. The Arabic inscription of good wishes is written in Kufic characters. Published: A.U. Pope, *Masterpieces of Persian Art*, 1945, Pl. 91B.

43. CUP

> *Molded ware with dark blue alkaline glaze*
> *Nishapur, Kashan (?), late 12th century*
> *Height: 3 1/2"*
> *Walters Art Gallery, Baltimore*

In this cup, the running animals have a background of leafy scrolls. Both are drawn with delicacy and liveliness. Nothing could show more clearly the change of spirit between the Samanid pottery of the 10th century and this of the Seljuk era of the 12th.

44. TANKARD

> *Molded with dark blue glaze, the handle restored*
> *Nishapur, 12th century*
> *Height: 6 5/8"*
> *Metropolitan Museum of Art, Rogers Fund*

It was definitely proved by the excavations of the Metropolitan Museum of Art which yielded fragments of molds and master molds that molded ware was made in Nishapur. There was considerable variety of style and quality among them. This particular example was not found by the expedition, but was purchased. Published: Dimand, M. S., *A Handbook of Muhammadan Art*, Metropolitan Museum of Art, 1944, p. 181, Fig. 113; Ettinghausen, R.E., "Evidence for the Identification of Kashan Pottery," in *Ars Islamica*, vol. III, 1936, pp. 68–69, Fig. 31; Lane, A., *Early Islamic Pottery*, 1947, Pl. 83b; *Survey of Persian Art*, vol. v, in color, Pl. 738.

45. DISH WITH FLAT RIM

> *So-called Lakabi carved ware*
> *12th century*
> *Diameter: 9 7/8"*
> *K. Rabenou Ltd., New York*

Blue, yellow, green, and purple are the colors used in this very distinctive group. Thus far, no wasters have been found to tell us accurately where the ware was made. It would appear that it came from one factory, but this is an assumption.

46. LION

Opaque turquoise-blue glaze, some restoration
12th-13th century
Height: 30"
Cincinnati Art Museum

This lion is one of the largest of this particular type of ceramic art. Another example, which is the image of a bird, once in the Sam A. Lewisohn Collection, is now in the Metropolitan Museum. The attraction of the two pieces depends rather on the color of the glaze than on the quality of the modeling. Published : A.U. Pope, *Survey of Persian Art*, vol. v, Pls. 766 and 677.

47. TILE

Opaque turquoise glaze
13th-14th century
Height: 9 1/2"
Metropolitan Museum of Art, bequest of William Milne Grinnell

The glaze is alkaline and has both copper and tin added to produce this opaque blue. It became fashionable at the end of the 12th century and continued for some time. Opaque blue glazed ware was reintroduced successfully by Hamadan potters in the present century.

48. JAR

Painted in black on relief decoration under a clear blue glaze
Kashan (?), 13th century
Height: 12 3/4"
Brooklyn Museum

Several jars of this type have survived. They so closely resemble each other that they would seem to come from one potter's factory. All have a band of Kufic with a foliated background. Fish, such as decorate the neck, form the major decoration of some vessels painted in black under an alkaline blue glaze. These are generally ascribed to Sultanabad, to the west of Kashan.

49. BOWL

White body and underglaze painted with stripes of black and blue
Kashan (?), Late 12th-early 13th century
Diameter: 7 7/8"
City Art Museum, St. Louis

Several bowls of this type were found in Gurgan, but they were probably imported from Kashan, although there is no actual proof of this. The shape, including the high foot ring, is typical of this ware. The body is mostly powdered quartz and the glaze is alkaline. Many lustered bowls are of this precise shape as are others painted in black under a blue glaze (see 52, 53). Published : *cf.* M. Bahrami, *Gurgan Faiences*, Pl. XIII.

50. WHITE BOWL

> *Painted in black under colorless alkaline glaze*
> *Kashan, late 12-early 13th century*
> *Diameter: 8 3/8"*
> *Mrs. Alice Heeramaneck, New York*

The decoration of underglaze painted bowls of this type was sometimes of the utmost simplicity, as in 49. In others there is more elaboration, though without producing a sense of overornamentation. The design in the bottom and the little plant forms on the outside are almost trademarks of this period.

51. BOWL

> *Pierced and painted in black under a clear blue glaze*
> *Kashan, late 12th-early 13th century*
> *Diameter: 8 7/8"*
> *Heeramaneck Galleries, New York*

Many bowls of this period were pierced to obtain transparencies which develop when clear glaze fills the holes. One very attractive group has a band of such decoration on a white ground and under a colorless glaze. In this example the glaze is colored and the pierced decoration supplemented by painted ornament. In addition, an inscription has been scratched out from a circular black band at the bottom.

52. JUG

> *Pierced outer shell decorated in black and blue under turquoise glaze.*
>   *The outside of the inner shell is plain blue*
> *Kashan, dated 612 A.H., A.D. 1215-16*
> *Height: 8"*
> *Metropolitan Museum of Art, Fletcher Fund*

A much practiced custom of Iranian potters of the 13th century was to enclose a vessel within a pierced hollow shell. A number of these have survived. None exhibits greater technical and artistic excellence than this particular example, which is dated A.D. 1215-16 (A.H. 612). The jug well repays close examination for its wealth of attractive detail incorporated in flowing stems and leaflike forms. Two bands of Persian poetry scratched out of the black ground contain this elaborate decoration. The jug used to be credited to Sultanabad, but it is now generally accepted as a product of the great ceramic center of Kashan. Formerly in the Macy Collection. Published: A. Lane, *Early Islamic Pottery*, London, 1947, Pl. 83b; M.S. Dimand, *Handbook of Muhammadan Art*, p. 180, Fig. 113; R.E. Ettinghausen, "Evidence for the Indentification of Kashan Pottery" in *Ars Islamica*, vol. III, 1936, pp. 68–69, Fig. 31.

53. BOWL

Painted in black under clear blue glaze
Kashan, late 12th-early 13th century
Diameter: 10"
John Herron Art Museum, Indianapolis

The bowl is reputed to have come from Gurgan, but if so it was surely imported. It is interesting to see that the artist felt it necessary to put spots on all his animals so that they do not stand out too starkly from the background. He has, however, taken care to vary the spotting on the animals so that the effect is not too repetitive.

54. BOWL

Painted in black under clear blue glaze
Kashan, early 13th century
Diameter: 9"
Nazli Heeramaneck, New York

This bowl is particularly interesting in that the motif of intertwined snakes with opposed heads appears on a similarly shaped luster bowl from Kashan, now in the Metropolitan Museum, which is dated 607 A.H., A.D. 1210.

55. PLATE

Luster painted on white and blue
Rayy, late 12th-early 13th century
Diameter: 14"
Philadeplhia Museum of Art, given by Henry P. McIlhenny

Cobalt blue decoration often figures in luster painted ware. In many the back of the vessel is blue, whereas this color does not appear on the face. The division of the design into sectors was an old tradition, but the potters of this time were not always as careful as here to keep the blue to the limits of the dividing lines. The Rayy potters also used blue to outline figures otherwise drawn in luster. Published : *Survey of Persian Art* (A.U. Pope, ed.) Pl. 648.

56. BOWL

Luster painted on white
Rayy, late 12th-early 13th century
Diameter: 14"
Cleveland Museum of Art, purchase from the J.H. Wade Fund

The bowl is one of several in which the design essentially consists of a man on horseback surrounded by foliation. In the earlier Nishapur styles the foliations are on the horse and not the background. Published : Baltimore, Johns Hopkins University (1940) Cat. no. 88; Howard Hollis, "Two Near Eastern Lustered Bowls," *Bulletin of The Cleveland Museum of Art* (November, 1944), pp. 158–60; Arther Lane, *Early Islamic Pottery*, London, 1947, p. 38; New York, Anderson Galleries, *Sale Catalogue of V. Everit Macy Collection* (January, 1938) no. 482; New York, Iranian Institute, *Guide to the Exhibition of Ceramic Art of the Near East* (1931) no. 52, p. 13; A.U. Pope, *Survey of Persian Art*, vol. v (London and New York, 1938–39) Pl. 633b.

57. CUP

Luster painted on white
Rayy, late 12th-early 13th century
Height: 5 1/8″
Seattle Art Museum, Eugene Fuller Memorial Collection

A group of luster vessels are distinguished by their very free and sketchy drawing of lively scenes, especially of horsemen. Very similar horsemen are to be seen on *minai* bowls of the same period. A peculiarity common to both is the indication of leaves by circular spots on both sides of curving stems.

58. BOWL

Decorated in gold luster on ivory white,
    with a palmette enclosed in a form resembling a pomegranate in red on the base
Kashan, mid-13th century
Diameter: 19 5/8″
Metropolitan Museum of Art, Fletcher Fund

The adornment of bowls by drawings of musicians was an inherited tradition practiced by the Sasanians several centuries prior to this time. In Islamic times, however, the human figures are not so prominent in the decorative scheme as both they and the background are often covered with tightly packed ornament. In this bowl the contrast is not between the human figures and the background, but between the circular zones, four of which are decorated with inscriptions in various hands. The exaggeration of the size of the lower part of the human face is typical of this period and suggests rather a gibbous moon than the full moon of poetry. Published : M.S. Dimand, *Islamic Pottery of the Near East, a picture book*. Metropolitan Museum of Art, 1936, Fig. 8; *Survey of Persian Art* (A.U. Pope, ed.) Pl. 711.

59. BOWL

Brown luster on white
Kashan, Muharram 609/June-July 1212
Diameter: 8 5/8″
Walters Art Gallery, Baltimore

Birds such as the pair that decorate this bowl very frequently appear in the designs of the Kashan potters. Published : R.E. Ettinghausen in *Ars Islamica*, vol. III, 1936, pp. 52, 68, Figs. 8 and 29.

60. FLOWER VASE

Overglaze painted in minai *with luster band at the top*
Rayy (?), 13th century
Height: 9″
Walters Art Gallery, Baltimore

Earlier examples of this type of vessel were made of blue glaze. This particular example, in which the spirit of the figures is so similar to that of the luster cup (57), is also related to it in that there is an inscription at the top which has been scratched out of a luster band. It is one of the several Iranian pieces which show clearly that *minai* and luster ware were sometimes, if not always, produced in the same place.

61. BOWL

Painted in minai *and embellished with gold*
Kashan (?), late 12th-early 13th century
Diameter: 8 1/4"
Walters Art Gallery, Baltimore

The art of painting in *minai* was developed to the utmost point of richness by the potters of the period in Iran. In this particular art they have never been matched in their own terms. One may prefer other types of ware, but no country produced better examples in this particular technique. In this bowl the elaboration has neither become confusing nor does it go beyond the point of acceptance. Published : J. Pijoan, *Summa Artis*, vol. XII, p. 314, Fig. 434.

62. BOWL

Overglaze painted on white ground in lavender, gray, pale green, and rust red. The inscription inside
    with black and green ornament and that outside in brown black.
Kashan, early 13th century
Diameter: 8 3/8"
Metropolitan Museum of Art, part purchase, part gift of Schiff Foundation

In contrast to the vivid colors of *minai* bowls, such as 61, others are more restrained. In these the fresh quality of the drawing is more stressed than richness of color and ornament. The scene here is easily recognized as the one in which Bahram Gur displays his skill in archery to his favorite. In case anyone should not know the name of the Sasanian hero, the potter has written it just behind the neck of the camel. Formerly in the Mortimer L. Schiff Collection. Published : M.S. Dimand, "New Accessions in Islamic Art" in the Metropolitan Museum of Art *Bulletin* N.S. vol. XVI, April, 1958, p. 228.

63. BOWL

Opaque turquoise with overglaze polychrome and gilt decoration
Kashan, 13th century
Diameter: 7 3/4"
Metropolitan Museum of Art, gift of Mr. and Mrs. A. Wallace Chauncey

These *minai* or enameled bowls did not always have a white ground. Turquoise was often used instead. The principal figure plays the lute, a word derived from the Arabic *el'ood*. Formerly in the Henry G. Leverthon Collection.

64. EWER

Bronze with silver inlay
Seljuk, 12th century
Height: 11 5/8"
Metropolitan Museum of Art, Huntley bequest

This form of ewer was a very common one in the 12th and 13th centuries. Around the body there is a Kufic inscription in high relief. There are other inscriptions engraved on the shoulder between bands, and also on the vertical foot ring. Some of the silver inlay is preserved. The loop beneath the spout suggests there was some kind of cover attached by a chain which is now missing. The influence of the design in metal work on that in pottery is very apparent (see 65). Published : Metropolitan Museum of Art *Bulletin*, April, 1960, p. 269 and illus.

[132]

65. EWER
   Luster and blue
   Kashan, 13th century
   Height: 12 1/2"
   Metropolitan Museum of Art

The comparison of this and the bronze ewer (64) clearly shows that there was a close relationship between pottery and metal work. The projections on the neck are reproduced and even the diagonal raised band at the root of the spout of the metal ewer is indicated by a white band on the ceramic copy.

66. TILE
   With inscription in relief and overglaze painted in blue and luster
   Kashan, 13th century
   Length: 15 3/4"
   Metropolitan Museum of Art

All the inscriptions are from the Koran (Suras 62 : 9, 34 : 11–13, 53 : 34–50). The inscriptions indicate that it came from a religious building, undoubtedly from a *mihrab*. From Kashan, *mihrabs* were exported to many different cities in Iran and some of them have been preserved more or less complete. They are composed of various elements including colonettes flanking the niche with surrounding bands of inscription.

67. TILE
   Luster painted with touches of green and blue
   Kashan, late 12th-early 13th century
   Height: 9 7/16"
   Museum of Fine Arts, Boston, Julia Knight Fox Fund

The tile is interesting for several reasons. It combines color and luster very skillfully, the drawing is masterly, and the scene itself depicts an event, and is not just a stock motif. The inscription on the white ground reads : "The departure of the Iranians from the fortress of Furad." Note the kettle drums to the right of the inscribed banners. Published : *Survey of Persian Art* (A.U. Pope, ed.), Pl. 706 (in color).

68. TILE
   Luster decoration
   Kashan, 13th century
   Height: 12 3/8"
   K. Rabenou Ltd., New York

The decoration of the tile is composed of ten seated figures, each with a halo and a flying dove between each couple.

69. TILE

Decorated in luster and an inscription with a blue background
14th century
Height: 8 1/8"
Walters Art Gallery, Baltimore

On tiles for secular use, the Kashan potters could let themselves have a little fun. This is one of two that have survived in which two men fight each other. Published : D. Guest and R.E. Ettinghausen, "The Iconography of a Kashan Luster Plate" in *Ars Orientalis*, vol. IV, p. 58, Pl. 22, Fig. 72.

70. TILE

Minai *with overglaze painting and gilding*
Kashan, 13th *century*
Height: 7 1/8"
Walters Art Gallery, Baltimore

In some tiles and bowls of the mid-13th century modeling was supplemented by overglaze painting. This combination, particularly with much gilding, tended to take away from the freshness of the earlier *minai* painting. Tiles such as this are decorated with scenes that show clearly that they were for secular purposes and not, as were many of the lustered tiles, for religious buildings. Formerly in the Alphonse Kann Collection.

71. ALBARELLO

Lajvardian ware, blue with overglaze painting in white, red, and gilt
Kashan, late 13th *century*
Height: 14 3/8" *with cover*
Metropolitan Museum of Art, gift of Mr. and Mrs. A. Wallace Chauncey

This particular ware was made in Kashan and the technique is described in the treatise of Abdul Qasim of Kashan written in A.D. 1301. It was employed not only for bowls and vessels, like this, but for tiles also. Formerly in the Henry G. Leberthon Collection. Published : M.S. Dimand, Metropolitan Museum of Art *Bulletin* N.S. vol. XVI, 1958, p. 228, illus. p. 235.

72. BOWL OF 14 SIDES

Painted in black and blue under colorless glaze, of a type called Sultanabad
Kashan (?), early 14th *century*
Diameter: 6 3/8"
Walters Art Gallery, Baltimore

The bowl is one of several of particularly fine quality with much delicacy in the drawing. It very closely resembles another in the collection of Sir Eldred Hitchcock (*see* A. Lane, *Islamic Pottery in the Collection of Sir Eldred Hitchcock*, 1956, no. 74). They surely were made by the same hand. The place of manufacture is not known for certain.

73. BOWL

Underglaze painted in dark blue, white, and black
Sultanabad type
First half of the 14th century
Diameter: 8 7/16"
Museum of Fine Arts, Boston, Marie Antoinette Fund and gift of Edward Jackson Holmes

Many vessels of a group, of which this is an excellent example, are marked by a very harmonious but restricted color scheme. Flying birds often appear in the decoration, but they are drawn in a thoroughly different spirit from those that appear on the luster wares of Kashan. The application of white slip tends to make the drawings of the foliage less precise than that in another group of which 72 is the best example, which may have been made in Kashan. This suggests another pottery, most probably in another city.

74. BOWL

Gray ground with white slip, cobalt blue, and umber
Diameter: 8 5/8"
Metropolitan Museum of Art, gift of Horace Havermeyer

This shape with a flat projecting rim and a sloping collar was exceedingly common in this 14th century ware. The sloping collar distinguishes it from the earlier wares. The twigs and outlines of umber were applied after the white slip. The alkaline glaze on the exterior is badly deteriorated giving the effect of iridescence.

75. BOWL

Imitation celadon, with three fish in relief inside and ribbed on the outside
Early 14th century
Diameter: 11 1/4"
Metropolitan Museum of Art, gift of Mrs. Horace Havemeyer, 1959,
*   in memory of her husband, Horace Havemeyer*

Celadon had been imported into Mesopotamia and Iran in the 9th century. It has been discovered in the Metropolitan Museum's excavations in both Kasr-i-abu Nasr near Shiraz and at Nishapur. In the 14th century it was being imitated in Iran. As in another example in the Victoria and Albert Museum, the fish have been touched up with spots of white slip under the glaze. (*See* A. Lane, *Late Islamic Pottery*, Pl. 86b.)

76. BOWL

Painted in black under blue glaze
Kubachi ware, North Iran, 15th century
Diameter: 12 3/8"
Metropolitan Museum of Art

This deep bowl is made of a gritty body covered with a white slip. The black underglaze has been scratched out with a fine point to produce the elaborate hairline minor decorations. These designs are very reminiscent of designs still to be seen on the textiles of Chinese Turkestan. The bowl is very similar to a bowl that belonged to D.K. Kelekian that is dated 875 A.H. (A.D. 1468). Published : A. Lane, *Later Islamic Pottery*, 1957, Pl. 20b.

77. BOTTLE

Blue and white. The base is glazed but unmarked
15th-16th century
Height: 18 1/2″
Metropolitan Museum of Art, Rogers Fund

The bottle is an interesting example of the confluence of Chinese, Iranian, and perhaps Turkish art. The body of the bottle, especially the ornament of inverted palmettes, is a design that is seen for a very considerable time in Chinese ceramics and that certainly continued into the 17th century in Iran. The animals, despite Chinese overtones (e.g., in the horns), continue the Iranian tradition—the leaping spotted animal for instance is not very different from some on the Macy jug (52). The glaze and the crackle are close to that of the so-called *Kubachi* ware. It is interesting to compare F.R. Martin, *Miniature Painting* (1912) vol. XI, Pls. 133, 137, and 252 from a manuscript executed for Shah Tamasp (1539–1543).

78. DISH

Blue and white
Kubachi ware, North Iran, 16th-17th century
Diameter: 12″

The central motif of this dish repeats fairly closely the most prominent motif to be seen in the late 15th century jar in the Timurid painting. The back of this dish is unusual in the night marish creatures with long fluked tails. The glaze has the large crackle and soft quality associated with *Kubachi* ware.

79. DISH

Blue and white
North Iran, end of 15th century
Diameter: 15 1/4″
Stuart C. Welch, Jr., Cambridge

This dish is related in style to one of the same shape in the Victoria and Albert Museum (A. Lane, *Later Islamic Pottery*) from Kubachi, but is more pleasing in the better balance of the design and the inclusion of the enlivening birds, which are Chinese rather than Iranian in inspriation.

80. DISH

Kubachi ware, polychrome
Northwest Iran (?), 17th century
Diameter: 13″
Walters Art Gallery, Baltimore

Many of these later *Kubachi* dishes show a weak, effeminate style which reflects all too well certain aspects of life in the Safavid captial of Isfahan, but some, of which this is an example, are decorated in a good lively manner.

[136]

81. DISH

Kubachi *ware. Cobalt blue, red and yellow ochre, and bright green; outlines in black.*
   Warm white ground under soft crackled glaze
Northwest Iran, 17th century
Diameter: 13 5/8"
Metropolitan Museum of Art

As is often the case with this ware, the white ground has become discolored. The two hunched figures in blue appear also in blue and white bowls made in Iran in imitation of Chinese wares.

82. BOWL

Kubachi *ware. Brown underglaze painting on bottom, with incised lotus flowers on the inside wall.*
   The exterior is slip-painted on dark brown ground. The white slip is touched with blue spots.
Northwest Iran, late 16th-early 17th century
Diameter: 10 7/8"
Metropolitan Museum of Art, gift of Mr. and Mrs. A. Wallace Chauncey

The bowl is a particularly fine example of early Safavid glazed ware. The incised design of lotus flowers is so subdued that it competes in no way with the elegance of the drawing of the singing bulbul (nightingale) perched on a leafy branch. Formerly in the Leverthon Collection.

83. CANDLE HOLDER

Blue and white
China, Cheng-te mark and period (1506-1521)
Height: 5 5/8"
Philadelphia Museum of Art, given by Mr. and Mrs. John Story Jenks

This candle holder of the early 16th century shows that the Chinese made export wares for Iran. On the piece is the following inscription: "I was loitering in a deserted place when suddenly I encountered a treasure."

84. DISH

Blue and white with incised band near the rim
Meshed, first half of 17th century
Diameter: 17 1/2"
Metropolitan Museum of Art, Rogers Fund

The large plate was probably made in Meshed where blue and white ware with a pure white body was produced. The outer border of the plate has an incised pattern that cannot show very clearly in a photograph. The animals, as is not unusual in this ware, are curiously soft; they lack the character and vigor of those in the old Iranian tradition. There is little reliance on a bold and expressive outline. Formerly in the Macomber Collection.

85. BOWL

Blue and white; blue fawn on base
17th century
Diameter: 11 1/16"
Walters Art Gallery, Baltimore

In spite of the attempt to incorporate certain Chinese characteristics, the potter has not followed the common custom of making an imitation Chinese mark on the base; instead, he has drawn a fawn in blue outline.

86. WINE BOTTLE

White with birds, clouds, and flowers in blue;
the medallions are filled with ochre yellow arabesques or with
a border of arabesques in white on white. Blue tassel mark on base.
Kirnan, early 17th century
Height: 13"
Metropolitan Museum of Art, Rogers Fund

The contrast between the strongly colored fluid drawing of the flying cranes and clouds and the stylized ornament is emphasized by the white and ochre color of the latter. This emphasis, however, by giving the blue the predominant role in the decoration, makes this daring combination an acceptable one. For a similar combination, see A. Lane, *Later Islamic Pottery*, Pl. 59a. It also appears in the 17th century artificial celadon, *op. cit.* Pl. 87a. The arabesques are similar in style to those on a Turkish (Isnik) mosque lamp from the Dome of the Rock, dated 956 A.H. (A.D. 1949). Published : M.S. Dimand, *A Handbook of Muhammedan Art*, p. 208, Fig. 136.

87. PANEL OF TILES

Isfahan, 17th century
Length: 6' 6"
Metropolitan Museum of Art, Rogers Fund

When Isfahan was the Safavid capital, i.e., during the 17th and early 18th centuries, there were a number of pavilions by the Chahar Bagh, of which only one remains in reasonably good condition, viz., the Chehil Setun. These were decorated with paintings and with panels of tiles of which this is a part of a larger one. They are interesting both for their subject matter and because they are colorful and gay. European influence is reflected by the dress of the young man on the left. Also to be observed are bottles, bowls, and cups that had a function in this *al fresco* party. Published : M.S. Dimand, *Handbook of Muhammedan Art*, Metropolitan Museum of Art 19; *see also*, Sarre, *Denkmaler persische Baukunst*, 1906–1909, Fig. 117.

88. PANEL OF TILES

Polychrome
Isfahan, 17th century
Height: 17 1/2"
Cleveland Museum of Art, John Huntington Collection

Many tiles and panels of tiles that were used to decorate pavilions and such secular buildings have survived. These tiles are square, unlike the earlier mosaic type in which many pieces, each of a separate color but not of the same shape, are assembled together. The colors are divided by heavy, clay-loaded manganese outlines, somewhat less pronounced than those employed in Achaemenian glazed bricks (*see color plate 15*). Many of these Safavid tile pictures are most attractive with their gay and beautiful colors. That color played a principal role at this time is proved by the unrealistic use of it. In some panels one sees, for example, green gazelles, which in no way seem shocking. Here two Ganymede boys are to be seen, one with a blue bottle of wine in his hand. The particular type of multi-colored turban worn here is often to be seen on plates of the so-called *Kubachi* type.

89. BOTTLE (KALIAN)
   Blue ground with slip-painting in white touched with yellow ochre
   Kirman, dated 1049 A.H./A.D. 1658-9
   Height: 11 1/2"
   Victoria and Albert Museum

Bottles of this shape were especially made for the water pipe (hubble bubble) so beloved by Turks and Persians. In 17th century Iran they were also made of luster ware. Published : A. Lane, *Later Islamic Pottery*, 1957, p. 106 and Pl. 88b.

90. BOTTLE (KALIAN)
   Polychrome on white with blue tassel mark on base
   Kirman, second half of the 17th century
   Height: 12 1/2"
   Victoria and Albert Museum

The bottle was used for smoking the water pipe, the long mouthpiece being inserted in the side and a metal container for the tobacco on the top. This is an excellent example of the polychrome ware of Kirman, which has, as is common, an imitation Chinese mark on the base. Published : A. Lane, *Later Islamic Pottery*, 1957, p. 82 and color plate D.

91. WINE BOTTLE
   Green glaze over relief decoration
   Isfahan (?), early 17th century
   Height: 14 3/8"
   Walters Art Gallery, Baltimore

The bottle is somewhat flattened and is decorated differently in relief on the two sides. On the side illustrated are three musicians in typical Safavid dress; on the other is an amorous scene. Sometimes the decoration suggests Chinese influence, but this is not the case with this bottle, which is thoroughly Persian. Small jars of this same type of ware are decorated with elaborate molded designs of foliated ornament. Orange-brown and amber are other colors of this monochrome glazed earthenware which is reputed to have been made in Isfahan.

92. FLASK
   Green glaze over relief decoration
   Isfahan (?), early 17th century
   Height: 8 5/8"
   Brooklyn Museum

Small bottles and flasks of this style were usually colored green or amber. The designs are charming and, as in this case, symmetrical on one side and asymmetrical on the other.

93. DISH

Celadon with white slip-painted decoration, in the center blue and white
Kirman, second half of the 17th century
Diameter: 18 1/8"
Philadelphia Museum of Art

In the 14th century the Iranian potters left their celadon almost plain, adding just a few blurred spots beneath the glaze. In the 17th century, the celadon ground was more intricately decorated and other colors were combined as in this very striking dish where the potter has boldy painted a design in blue and white that gives the impression of being an inset tile. Published : Survey of Persian Art, (A.U. Pope, ed.). Pl. 802; A. Lane, *Later Islamic Pottery*, 1957, p. 106, no illus.

94. BOWL

Slip-painted celadon with cobalt spots
Northwest Iran (?), 17th century
Diameter: 9 5/8"
Walters Art Gallery

This deep bowl has a floral design in the center and around the rim. More floral designs on the exterior are similarly painted in white slip on the sharp celadon green which has been affected by the cobalt blue spots.

95. WINE BOTTLE

Luster on blue
Second half of the 17th century
Height: 10"
Cincinnati Art Museum, given in honor of Mr. and Mrs. Chas. F. Williams by their children

Luster painting, which enjoyed such a vogue in Persia and achieved such heights of excellence in the 12th and early 13th centuries and died out in the 15th, reappeared once more in Safavid times. The designs have no relationship to the earlier ware and, though produced at a time when there was much Oriental influence, are very Persian in character. Some bottles are lustered on a white ground, others are particolored, white and brilliant blue with luster over both.

96. EWER

Incised decoration on white under colorless glaze
Height: 9 5/16"
Art Institute of Chicago, Mary Jane Gunsaulus Collection

Much of the late Safavid ware which is deceptively like porcelain is decorated with incised patterns that, though repetitive, are drawn in a free and spirited manner. Many of the vessels are well shaped so that they have an elegance that is not always characteristic of Iranian ceramics. This ewer is unmarked on the base.

[140]

97. EWER

Luster decoration on white
Second half of the 17th century
Height: 5 1/2"
Metropolitan Museum of Art, bequest of Isaac D. Fletcher

In the 17th and 18th centuries luster was used for decorating bowls, ewers, and small cups without handles. The designs are pretty rather than impressive and often incorporate trees, charming but unreal, that harbor singing birds and shelter couchant deer.

98. BOWL

Incised decoration of lotus flowers on white under colorless glaze. Blue mark on the base
Kirman (?), 17th-18th century
Diameter: 7 7/8"
Metropolitan Museum of Art, gift of W. R. Valentiner

Persian white wares of the 17th and 18th centuries are often very charming and have not had their due meed of praise. A number of them are elegant in both shape and design; the ornament is sometimes incised to such an extent that the outlines that form the decoration are translucent. The body is white and almost vitrified.

99. BOWL

Enamel-painted polychrome
Shiraz, dated 1846
Diameter: 16 3/8"
Victoria and Albert Museum

The bowl is signed : "The work of the most miserable Ali Akbar of Shiraz 1262." The bowl reflects the Kajar style known to us mostly by lacquered pen boxes and paintings. This combines certain features of both, the bouquets of flowers and the portraits with curtains drawn aside. Published : A. Lane, *Later Islamic Pottery*, 1957, Pl. 62b.

(NOT ILLUSTRATED)

75a. BOWL WITH TWO FISH

Lung Ch'uan ware
China, 10th-13th century
Diameter: 8 1/4
Nathan V. Hammer, New York

This Chinese celadon bowl has all the brilliant, hard, precise qualities that are lacking in Iranian pottery. The pottery of each country affected the other at certain times, but rarely can the one be mistaken for the other.

77a. MINIATURE PAINTING

> *Page from Khawar-nama, showing ceramics of the 15th century in recessed niches*
> *Timurid, painted in Shiraz about 1477*
> *Stuart C. Welch, Jr., Cambridge*

a. As can be seen clearly, the vessels in the niches are markedly Chinese in appearance. A great deal of blue and white Timurid pottery has been found in Samarkand, but it has not been adequately published.

90a. BOTTLE

> *Molded and decorated in turquoise, lavender, purple, and yellow glazes*
> *17th century* A.D.
> *Height: 12″*
> *Victoria and Albert Museum*

a. During the Safavid period there were many exotically shaped vessels and a great variety of color was used to decorate them. Related to this, of finer workmanship, but more restrained in color, are others of monochrome. Published : A. Lane, *Later Islamic Pottery*, 1957, p. 71, Pl. 92.

BIBLIOGRAPHY

BAHRAMI, M. *Gurgan Faiences.* Cairo, 1949.

——. "Contribution à l'étude de la céramique Musulmane de l'Iran," *Athar-é Iran,*" vol. III (1938), pp. 209-229.

BERGHE, L. V. *Archéologie de l'Iran ancien.* Leiden, 1959.

DIMAND, M. S. *A Handbook of Muhammedan Art.* Metropolitan Museum of Art, New York, 1958.

ETTINGHAUSEN, R. "Evidence for the Identification of Kashan Pottery," *Ars Islamica,* vol. III (1936), pp. 44-75.

GHIRSHMAN, R. *Fouilles de Sialk,* vol. I (1938); vol. II (1939).

GODARD, Y. "Pièces datées de céramique de Kashan à décor lustre," *Athar-é Iran,* vol. II (1937), pp. 309-337.

HOBSON, R. L. *A Guide to the Islamic Pottery of the Near East.* British Museum, London, 1932.

JAKOBSEN, K. *Islamische Keramik.* Museum für Kunst und Gewerbe, Hamburg, 1959.

KOECHLIN, R. "Les Céramiques Musulmanes de Suse au Musée du Louvre," *Mémoires de la Mission Archéologique de Perse,* vol. XIX (1928).

KÜHNEL, E. "Dated Persian Lustred Pottery," *Eastern Art,* vol. III (1931), pp. 221-236.

LANE, A. *Early Islamic Pottery.* London, 1947.

——. *Later Islamic Pottery.* London, 1957.

——. "The so-Called 'Kubachi' Wares of Persia," *Burlington Magazine,* vol. LXXV (1939), pp. 156-162.

PEZARD, M. *La céramique archaïque de l'Islam et ses origines.* Paris, 1920.

POPE, A. U., ed. *Survey of Persian Art,* vol. II (1939); vol. V (1938). London and New York.

RITTER, H., RUSKA, J., SARRE, F., and WINDERLICH, R. *Orientalische Steinbücher und persische Fayencetechnik.* Istanbul, 1935.

WILKINSON, C. K. "The Glazed Pottery of Nishapur and Samarkand," *Bulletin,*

(WILKINSON. *continued*)

Metropolitan Museum of Art, vol. xx (1961), pp. 102-115.

——. "Fashion and Technique in Persian Pottery," *Bulletin*, Metropolitan Museum of Art, vol. vi (1947), pp. 99-104.

—— (with Hauser, W., and Upton, J. M.). "The Iranian Expedition, 1936," [Nishapur], *Bulletin*, Metropolitan Museum of Art, vol. xxii, sec. ii, no. 10 (1937) pp. 3-38.

——. "The Iranian Expedition, 1937," [Nishapur], *Bulletin*, Metropolitan Museum of Art, vol. xxxiii, sec. ii, no. 11 (1938), pp. 3-23.

—— (with Hauser, W.). "The Museum's Excavations at Nishapur," *Bulletin*, Metropolitan Museum of Art, vol. xxxvii (1942), pp. 83-119.

LENDERS TO THE EXHIBITION

Art Institute of Chicago
Mr. and Mrs. Arthur Babakhanian
(*through the Metropolitan Museum of Art*)
Brooklyn Museum
Cincinnati Art Museum
City Art Museum of St. Louis
Cleveland Museum of Art
Mr. and Mrs. John de Menil
Richard Ettinghausen
(*through the Baltimore Museum of Art*)
Nathan V. Hammer, New York
Mrs. Alice Heeramaneck, New York
Heeramaneck Galleries, New York
Mr. and Mrs. Nazli Heeramaneck, New York
John Herron Art Institute, Indianapolis
Charles D. Kelekian, New York
Mahdi Mahboubian, New York
Metropolitan Museum of Art, New York
Museum of Fine Arts, Boston
Philadelphia Museum of Art
K. Rabenou, Ltd., New York
Dr. and Mrs. William K. Simpson
(*through the Metropolitan Museum of Art*)
University Museum, Philadelphia
Walters Art Gallery, Baltimore
Stuart C. Welch, Cambridge, Massachussetts
Mr. and Mrs. Lester Wolfe
(*through the Metropolitan Museum of Art*)